5TO

ALLEN COUNTY PUBLIC LIBRARY

FRIENDS
OF ACPL

599 M13
McClung
Lost wild worlds

S0-BHW-409

NOV 19 '76

LOST WILD WORLDS

Books by Robert M. McClung

Aquatic Insects and How They Live
Bees, Wasps, and Hornets and How They Live
Gypsy Moth, Its History in America
Lost Wild America
Mice, Moose, and Men, How Their Populations Rise and Fall
Samson, Last of the California Grizzlies
and others

The Story of
Extinct and Vanishing Wildlife
of the Eastern Hemisphere

LOST WILD WORLDS

BY ROBERT M. McCLUNG

with illustrations by Bob Hines

William Morrow and Company
New York 1976

Copyright © 1976 by Robert M. McClung
All rights reserved. No part of this book may be reproduced or utilized in
any form or by any means, electronic or mechanical, including photocopy-
ing, recording or by any information storage and retrieval system, without
permission in writing from the Publisher. Inquiries should be addressed to
William Morrow and Company, Inc., 105 Madison Avenue., New York, N. Y.
10016.
Printed in the United States of America.
1   2   3   4   5   6   7   8   9   10

Library of Congress Cataloging in Publication Data

McClung, Robert M.
  Lost wild worlds.

  Bibliography: p.
  Includes index.
  SUMMARY: A survey of the past and present wildlife of Europe, Asia,
Africa, Madagascar and the islands of the Indian Ocean, the Malay Archi-
pelago, Australia, and New Zealand. Includes a discussion on the future of
wildlife.
  1. Wildlife conservation—History.   2. Animals and civilization—History.
3. Rare animals.   4. Extinct animals.   [1. Wildlife conservation—History.
2. Animals and civilization.   3. Rare animals.   4. Extinct animals]   I. Hines,
Robert W.   II. Title.
QL81.7.M3   591'.04'2091811   76-25851
ISBN 0-688-22090-8
ISBN 0-688-32090-2 lib. bdg.

1929835

CONTENTS

ACKNOWLEDGMENTS

The works of many naturalists, conservationists, historians, and geographers dating from more than two thousand years ago until today, as well as hundreds of current books, periodicals, articles, and news items have been consulted in the preparation of this book. I gratefully acknowledge my indebtedness to the authors of all of them, many of whom are listed in the index.

Dr. James A. Oliver, Director of the New York Aquarium, kindly reviewed the reptile accounts. Joseph Bell, Curator of Ornithology at the New York Zoological Park, patiently answered various questions, as did Philip DuMont of the Fish and Wildlife Service. My two sons have read portions of the manuscript and added their comments and views. Reference librarians and other staff at the Amherst Town Library, the Robert Frost

11

Library at Amherst College, and the Morrill Science Library at the University of Massachusetts, all were invariably interested and diligent in helping to track down materials. The accounts in the text of the Asiatic deer, tiger, gorilla, crocodile, and platypus, all first appeared in somewhat different form in *Defenders,* the magazine of Defenders of Wildlife. I thank all of the above individuals and organizations for their assistance.

William Bridges, Curator of Publications Emeritus of the New York Zoological Society; George Crossette, former Director of Geographic Research at the National Geographic Society; and Dr. Robert B. Whitney, Professor Emeritus of Chemistry at Amherst College, have all read the manuscript in its entirety, pointing out various inaccuracies and contributing countless helpful suggestions. I thank them for their valuable contributions. Any mistakes that may remain are my own, as is the responsibility for all of the statements and expressed opinions.

Finally, I deeply appreciate the care and help of my editors, Connie Epstein and Lynda Barber, who have guided the book through its many stages; of Cynthia Basil, designer of the book and creator of the jacket and maps; of Bob Hines, whose attractive and expert illustrations add so much to the appearance of the book; and of my wife, Gale, whose encouragement, advice, criticism, and material aid throughout the project have been of immeasurable help.

FOR GALE, BILL, AND TOM.

Accuse not nature! She hath done her part; Do thou but thine! and be not diffident of wisdom; she deserts thee not, if thou dismiss not her.   John Milton

FOREWORD

"It really is a pity," observed the noted French missionary-naturalist Abbé Armand David more than a century ago, "the education of the human species did not develop in time to save the irremediable destruction of so many species which the Creator placed on our Earth to live beside man, not merely for beauty, but to fulfill a useful role necessary for the economy of the whole."

One of the species that Père David may have been thinking of when he wrote these words was the great auk, a nineteenth-century victim of man's ruthlessness and greed. The last recorded specimen of this large flightless bird was clubbed to death on June 4, 1844, by a collector on remote Eldey Island off the coast of Iceland.

15

On March 6, 1971, a mounted great auk—killed in Iceland in 1821—was sold at Sotheby's auction house in London for $21,600. The successful bidder was Dr. Finnyr Gudmunesson, Director of the Icelandic Museum of National History in Reykjavik.

Will mounted museum specimens such as this become the final destiny for today's endangered wildlife, too? Or will they be reduced to a few living specimens carefully preserved in zoos or managed and protected in game preserves and parks? If so, the world will be a far worse place to live; man himself will be something less than human.

The World Wildlife Fund, an international organization devoted to preserving endangered wildlife, notes that at least forty species of mammals have become extinct since the year 1600, and that ninety-four species of birds have suffered the same fate. They further report that more than nine hundred species and subspecies of animals will inevitably disappear within the next few years unless effective steps are taken to save them.

An ominous warning, indeed. But even more ominous is the knowledge that the *pace* at which this is happening quickens year by year. "During the past 150 years the rate of extermination of mammals has increased 55-fold," according to Dr. Lee M. Talbot, an ecologist with the Smithsonian Institution in Washington, D.C. "If the killing goes on at this pace, in about 30 years all of the remaining 4062 species of mammals will be gone." Birds, reptiles, fish—all living things—face this same threat, as suitable habitat shrinks and the environment becomes more polluted each year.

Perched at the summit of the living pyramid, *Homo sapiens* faces the same fate, for not even man can destroy the environment he needs to support life and escape the consequences.

How has such a situation come about? The answer lies with

man's exploding population, and what is happening to the earth as a result. "Mankind is endangered by a crisis of planetary proportions," asserts population expert Richard Falk. "This crisis has emerged out of the interplay between a machine technology and a rising population. . . . The endangered planet arises in part because our technological abilities are evolving so much more rapidly than our abilities to solve social and political problems."

Wild animals are among the first victims resulting from man's dramatic ability to master and change the natural world. Many people either do not know how their activities may affect wildlife and the living earth, or they simply don't care. Many others place their own economic well-being above everything else. Motivated by greed, they ruthlessly pollute the land and seas with industrial wastes and poisons, destroy the environment, and exploit wildlife.

The account that follows tells briefly of man's rise to civilization, how he spread over the earth and explored it, and how he finally came to dominate it and alter it to his own uses. Through narrative accounts of wildlife species, continent-by-continent, this book relates how man has brought about the extinction of many kinds of wildlife and endangered the survival of others. It also tells how organizations and individuals of goodwill in many countries are endeavoring to reverse these destructive trends and save our fellow creatures.

The animals selected for narrative discussion were chosen for a variety of reasons. Some examples show how destructive forces can cause a once-flourishing species to dwindle until it becomes either endangered or extinct; others illustrate how positive forces exerted by governments, conservation organizations, and individuals can work to save a threatened species. Some species have been saved through enlightened management in the wild, some by strict enforcement of protective laws. Other critically endangered forms are being preserved by safeguarding a nucleus of captive breeding stock in zoos or private game reserves. A few benefit from newly developed scientific techniques. Several major animal groups, such as the big cats and whales, are the objects of worldwide campaigns aimed at arousing public opinion in their behalf and creating sanctuaries for them to insure their numbers.

"The campaign to save the tiger," the *New York Times* has observed, "does not remotely imply failure to recognize the crying social needs of that other animal—man. But the saving of tigers —and whales and wolves, for that matter—is more than a cultural and esthetic compulsion. All the flora and fauna of the earth form an endlessly complex web of life, which man tears at his peril."

WHERE LIES TOMORROW?

One way or another, whether civilizations collapsed, were over-thrown or were victims of disaster or failure, the answer always has been that the earth itself, the source of all life, was the eventual reality and the place to find certainty and ultimate truth. . . . Nature's purpose, so far as we understand purpose at all, is to perpetuate life, not to destroy it, to strengthen life, not to weaken it, to garland and fructify the earth, not blight and devastate it.   Editorial, The New York Times

ARCTIC OCEAN

EUROPE

ASIA

ATLANTIC OCEAN

PACIFIC
OCEAN

AFRICA

MALAY ARCHIPELAGO

INDIAN
OCEAN

AUSTRALIA

MADAGASCAR

NEW ZEALAND

EASTERN HEMISPHERE

Woe to them that join house to house, that lay field to field, till there be no place, that they may be placed alone in the midst of the earth. Isaiah

1

MAN'S RISE TO DOMINANCE

Be fruitful, and multiply and replenish the earth, and subdue it: and have dominion over the fish of the sea, and over every living thing that moveth upon the earth.

Taken literally, this quotation from Genesis would seem to be a clear direction for *Homo sapiens* to rule the earth and all its creatures—as man is doing today—and make of it what he wants. Throughout history many people have so understood it. Most modern Biblical scholars, however, would interpret the passage to indicate more man's *responsibility* for the stewardship and well-being of his fellow inhabitants of the earth, rather than his dominion over them.

Read in its entirety, Genesis is a beautiful story, telling in a

21

simple explanatory way of the creation of the earth, the emergence of life upon it, and the rise of all the various life forms, with each day of the legend representing many millions of years. Man, according to the story, was formed on the sixth day of creation. All other living things had been created before him.

Paleontologists, scientists who study prehistoric life, tell us that the last dinosaur on earth died some 70 million or more years ago. With its passing, the Golden Age of Reptiles, which lasted some 120 million years or more, also ended. It was then —on that symbolic sixth day—that the mammals emerged.

The first mammals, tiny insect eaters, had appeared long before, and so had the first ancient birds. Both had sprung from reptilian ancestors. When the primitive little mammals were freed from the dominance of the ruling reptiles, they began to specialize and evolve in many different directions. The Age of Mammals—the age in which we live today—had begun.

The earth gradually cooled during the millions of years that followed, while representatives of all the groups of modern mammals were evolving. This long cooling process finally culminated in the Pleistocene epoch, or Ice Age, more than a million years ago, when great sheets of glacial ice pushed outward from the poles and covered much of the earth.

The First Men

Four times the great Arctic ice cap crunched southward, covering all of northern Europe, Asia, and North America during the coldest times, then retreated back toward the North Pole during intervening periods of milder weather. An astounding variety of Ice Age mammals flourished during the Pleistocene: mammoths and mastodons, woolly rhinoceroses, giant bison, horses, camels and deer, among others. It was during this period also that modern man was evolving.

According to the latest findings, modern man's hominid ancestors—humanlike creatures that walked upright and possessed other human traits—evolved nearly four million years ago. Fossil remains of early man, scientifically dated as between 3,350,000 and 3,750,000 years old, have recently been uncovered near Olduvai Gorge in Tanzania, East Africa. These, as reported by Dr. Mary Leakey early in 1976, appear to represent the genus *Homo,* or true man. Many paleontologists, on the basis of this and earlier evidence, believe that the first true men evolved in Africa. Others argue that the process of hominization occurred among several apelike creatures throughout Africa and Eurasia. But wherever our ancestors arose, among the first of them that we would recognize as fellow human beings were those who appeared on the African plains over a half million years ago.

Arriving in Europe two hundred thousand or so years ago, these primitive men, whom we now call *Homo erectus* (man who walks upright), lived together in small bands. They had smaller brains than modern man, but they knew how to use fire, fashioned crude weapons from stone, and hunted wild animals for food. About one hundred thousand years ago, they were succeeded in Europe by Neanderthal man.

The best known of all the prehistoric men, the Neanderthal, had a brain as large as modern man's. Standing only about five feet tall, he was heavily muscled, short-legged, and beetle-browed. He lived in caves during the coldest periods and may have built primitive shelters from animal hides or branches of trees. He used fire both to warm himself and cook his food, and he considerably advanced the art of making and using weapons of stone and flint. A skilled hunter, Neanderthal man captured small animals in snares, and with his spears and axes killed animals as big as the woolly mammoth and rhinoceros after they had fallen into natural pits or become mired in bogs. He buried his dead and had the beginnings of a crude religion.

Some thirty or forty thousand years ago, Neanderthal man

disappeared quite suddenly, swallowed up by the coming of a more advanced relative: Cro-Magnon man.

Cro-Magnon Man Appears

Except for their great age, the skeletal remains of Cro-Magnon man cannot be distinguished from the remains of men living today. Cro-Magnon man's brain was just as big as our brain and equally as capable of reasoning and solving complex problems. But Cro-Magnon man did not have all of the accumulated discoveries of science to back up his actions, as we have today. Already an expert hunter and toolmaker, however, he was beginning to accumulate basic knowledge that would form the groundwork for all of our sophisticated science and technology. The more he learned, the quicker his knowledge and techniques expanded. This primitive man represented a vital step on the long and fateful journey that led to modern technological man.

As the great ice sheets ebbed and flowed over the past thirty to forty thousand years, Cro-Magnon man populated much of the Old World. Sometime during that period he migrated from Asia to North America over the Bering land bridge that lay exposed between the two great land masses. This bridge was exposed when the vast ice sheets locked up such an enormous amount of water that the levels of the oceans were lowered.

Cro-Magnon man perfected the art of making weapons of stone as no other men had done before him. Working with painstaking patience and skill, he fashioned delicate but deadly blades and spearheads from flint and quartz. He made harpoon heads with fine sharp edges and many barbs, and he created effective spear throwers from reindeer antlers. The most skillful and deadly hunter the world had yet known, Cro-Magnon man hunted mammoths and rhinoceroses, primitive horses, reindeer, and many other animals during the colder periods. In warmer weather he pursued deer and bison and wild cattle on the European steppes and in the forests. Some modern authorities believe that because of his success at hunting, he was responsible for the extinction of many of these big game animals of the late Pleistocene. The skeletal remains of some one thousand or more mammoths found at Predmost, Czechoslovakia, and great bone heaps near Solutré, France, containing the remains of many thousands of horses are awesome proof of early man's hunting abilities.

As befitted his role as hunter and predator, Cro-Magnon man worshipped the wild creatures that he depended upon for food, shelter, and life. Medicine men, or shamans, dressed in animal skins and covered their faces with animal masks during religious ceremonies and festivals. They hoped to gain favor with the spirits of the animals they represented so that the tribe would have successful hunts.

By the light of flickering torches, gifted Cro-Magnon artists painted animal shapes on the walls of caves. Mixing clay of various shades with mineral oxides and charcoal, these early artists fashioned pigments of red, yellow, brown, and black. They then mixed the pigments with animal fat to bind the colors and spread them on cave ceilings and walls either by hand or with some kind of crude brush or crayon. Some archaeologists believe that the pigments were sometimes blown in powder form through hollow tubes of bone. Their vivid paintings depicted wild animals, as well as primitive hunters making their kills of bison, deer, rhinoceroses, and horses. These decorated caves were Cro-Magnon man's temples dedicated to the hunt.

In 1940, the famous cave in Lascaux, France, was discovered by young boys when their little dog fell into a crack in the earth. In an attempt to rescue their pet, they dug the opening wider and entered a vast cavern several hundred feet long. Awestruck, they gazed at hundreds of paintings depicting animals of the Ice Age.

The Advance of Civilization

Bit by bit, Cro-Magnon man began to change his nomadic life as he learned different methods of utilizing the land and animals around him. Some men stayed by the shores of lakes and became fishermen, fashioning nets and traps and building crude canoes and boats. Others learned how to grow crops and began to live in one place instead of wandering from one area to another. Man also began to domesticate wild sheep, cattle, and horses, and many tribes were supported by the meat, milk, and wool that their stock produced.

These prehistoric men eventually learned how to use metals such as bronze and iron instead of stone for their weapons and tools. The use of metal was the beginning of a new era. Man was fast becoming civilized. Those living by the sea built larger boats in which they could take long voyages. Trade and commerce with neighboring peoples began to flourish. As man advanced, so did his arts and religion.

A host of early Old World civilizations rose and fell. In the lands bordering the Mediterranean, they culminated in the glories of ancient Egypt and Greece, and ultimately in the power of Rome; in Asia they led to highly developed civilizations in Persia, India, and China. All of these expanding cultures began to exert powerful pressures and changes on the environment.

Man's swift rise from those early beginnings to his dominance in today's world is well documented in recorded history. In the continuous struggle for power, many wars were fought as man increased his knowledge and applied skills. In the eighteenth century, Western man made the great scientific breakthrough known as the Industrial Revolution. This revolution was the result of thousands of years of accumulated knowledge that led to a rapid series of inventions. Man learned how to harness steam and to manufacture many kinds of products more efficiently and cheaply. And along with the escalating technology, advances in agricultural knowledge and medicine allowed more people in the Western world to live longer.

The human population of the earth, which was almost stationary or rose very slowly during the preceding million years, suddenly began to increase in startling fashion. From a half billion people in 1650, the world population of *Homo sapiens* doubled to one billion in 1850, just 200 years later. Only 80 years were needed for the next population doubling to some two billion in 1930. Today's world population is about four billion, with prospects of doubling again in the next 35 years. And the more people there are, the more pressures are exerted upon our planet Earth, thereby increasing the dangers to all living things—including man himself.

Technological Man

As man increases in numbers, he changes the earth more and more. The last great wilderness areas of the world—the Amazon jungles, the Alaskan tundra, the forests of New Guinea —all are being attacked by eager exploiters. Newly emerging African and Asian nations are working feverishly to clear lands for more crops and development. As a result, the wildlife of every continent is losing more and more of the natural habitat that it needs for survival. The human demand for food and goods is responsible for increased chemical pollution of the lands and seas every year. In the process, countless forms of wildlife are being killed or threatened—and even man himself. "A new generation is being raised," says ecologist Barry Commoner,

"—with DDT in their fat, carbon monoxide in their systems and lead in their bones. That is technological man."

We used to worry about enthusiastic hunters killing off wildlife species. One Englishman, Lord Ripon, who died in 1923 at the age of seventy-one, was credited with killing 500,000 game birds and animals—or about 67 creatures for every shooting day of his life! He was recognized as the finest game shot in the country, but he was also known, justifiably, as the Game Hog of Dallowgill. And it was just a few years ago that one Indian maharajah remarked that he had killed 1,150 tigers. Both of these hunters killed merely for what they called "sport."

There are still wholesale killers of game today, but the usual motive for killing wildlife on a large scale is based on economic gain. The world's whale populations continue to dwindle as the slaughter of the great sea mammals for their meat and oil continues, aided by sophisticated radar and tracking devices, helicopters, and speedy killer boats armed with powerful harpoon guns. Kangaroos compete with domestic livestock for grass, and as a result they are killed by uncounted thousands in Australia, where one rancher alone recently boasted of shooting 20,000 on his spread in four years. Crocodilians are being slain for their hides, as are many of the big spotted cats.

Today, on every continent, man is taking more and more of the land that wildlife needs and adapting it for his own uses to meet the needs of expanding populations. What is the solution to the dilemma of a rising human population with all its requirements, while safeguarding the environment and the rights of wildlife in a changing world? In 1972, the world's first United Nations Conference on the Human Environment was held at Stockholm. The differing points of view between the rich and the poor nations, between technologically advanced and underdeveloped countries, proved in many cases to be an almost impossible obstacle to meaningful discussion.

The rich nations of the West expressed their alarm at the rising populations of many of the poorer nations, and they predicted that unprecedented famine will soon result unless population increases are curbed very quickly. The less-developed countries, for their part, blame the advanced Western nations for selfish and conspicuous waste of food and natural resources —much of it at the expense of the poor nations—in order to maintain their accustomed high standards of living. "Industrialized countries put the blame on those who have not yet industrialized for not controlling the growth of their populations," observed Mobutu Sese Seko, President of Zaire, when he addressed the twelfth General Assembly of the International Union for the Conservation of Nature and Natural Resources (IUCN), which met in his country in September, 1975; "and they emphasize the dangers of this, especially in terms of food shortage. At the same time, however, they forget that their own populations, although representing only one third of mankind, consume 90 percent of the planet's resources. Their planes and their cars use up twice as much oxygen as does the entire population of the world. And it is because of them that the seas today are polluted. . . ."

Developing nations such as Zaire understandably want their fair share of the world's riches; they want a higher living standard for their peoples too and are fiercely determined to achieve it.

The simple truth is that the earth cannot begin to produce all of the food and other resources necessary to support the peoples of the world in anything like the luxurious standard of living now enjoyed by the majority of Americans and Western Europeans. The conference emphasized this fact, among others, and several common areas of concern were noted in spite of the radically different points of view.

Most of the world is at least aware of the problems brought

about by rising populations and dwindling resources. What to do about them is the crucial question man now faces. In answering that dilemma he must recognize that the animal and vegetable life of the earth—their complex relationships and their preservation—are closely bound up with his own ultimate well-being.

No man is an island, entire of itself; Every man is a piece of the continent, a part of the main. . . . Any man's death diminishes me, because I am involved in mankind; And therefore never send to know for whom the bell tolls; it tolls for thee.   John Donne

2

EUROPE, CRADLE OF WESTERN CIVILIZATION

After the last great retreat of the glaciers, some ten thousand years ago, man found southern Europe a promising land in which to begin his civilization. Most of temperate Europe was still a forest wilderness; but once cleared, it would prove to be fertile, ideal for agriculture. In those days, however, it was an unknown land, home of many barbarian tribes and the wild animals that they hunted—wild horses and cattle, bison, deer, bear, beaver, and fur-bearing animals of many kinds. To the southeast, it merged with the steppes, endless plains stretching from the Caspian and Black Seas eastward into central Asia. All of this vast area of temperate Europe was unaffected by man's

PLAND

Leningrad

Volga River

Moscow

UNION OF SOVIET SOCIALIST REPUBLICS
(Russia)

Ural Mountains

Volga River

UKRAINE

CRIMEA

CASPIAN SEA

Danube River

BLACK SEA

CE

Athens

influence until approximately two thousand years ago, when civilization in the form of Roman legions arrived.

Civilization had come much earlier to parts of southern Europe, and the shores of the Mediterranean were among the first lands to be scarred by man. Until the rise of the Greeks, however, those marks were still minimal. "Eight thousand years ago the world of the Mediterranean had a vastly different aspect from the one it bears today," the French naturalist François Bourlière has noted. "Where Athens now stands on its barren hills, there grew a forest of oak and pine. . . . From the gateway of the Atlantic to western Asia, the Mediterranean area, the 'middle land' of our forebears, was covered with a blanket of forest which even extended to some of the land we know today as total desert along the North African coast."

The Phoenicians and Greeks

The Phoenicians, well-established at the eastern end of the Mediterranean, had already explored the shores of the great land-locked sea, and by 1400 B.C. they had colonized many coastal areas. In the eighth century B.C., the Phoenicians established Carthage as a powerful outpost on the rim of North Africa. During this same period the power and greatness of the ancient Greeks was emerging, and with them came an expansion of man's knowledge of his world.

About 320 B.C., Pytheas, an adventuresome Greek scientist and navigator, who was a citizen of Massilia (Marseilles), sailed his ship through the Pillars of Hercules—the Rock of Gilbraltar in Europe and the promontory of Jebel Musa in Africa—and out into the open Atlantic. Heading northward along the coast of the Iberian Peninsula, he is said to have sailed his ship all the way around Britain, bringing back to his wondering countrymen tales of the barbarians that inhabited that strange land to

the north. In 329 B.C., Philip of Macedonia was extending
Western man's knowledge of Asia, leading his armies eastward
to the headwaters of the Indus River. In the process, he battled
Oriental princes who opposed him with battalions of elephants.
Greek power was at its zenith at this time, with the influence of
Greek civilization being felt throughout the Western world and
into Egypt and Asia as well.

Roman Civilization   1929835

Greek power began to fade several centuries afterward, and
gradually many of the Grecian colonies were taken over and
absorbed by the Romans, who were starting to establish one of
the great empires of history. Especially good at organization and
engineering, the Romans borrowed whatever they needed of
science and the arts from Greece and other civilizations. They
then adapted the knowledge for their own needs. By 290 B.C.,
the Romans had finally defeated their rivals, the Carthaginians,
and thereafter were the undisputed rulers of the Mediterranean
regions. Africa and Asia lay open to their armies and so did
the as yet unknown interior of barbarian Europe.

In 58 B.C., the Roman general Gaius Julius Caesar marched
into Gaul—now France and the low countries—and quickly
conquered it. He followed this victory by invading Britain, in
55 B.C., and inaugurating a long period of Roman rule there.
The next two-hundred-year period saw the extension of Roman
power and rule over a great empire, extending from Scotland
in the north to the Mediterranean rim of Africa in the south,
and from Spain through all of western Europe to Egypt and the
Near East. Throughout this vast territory the Romans bestowed
the Pax Romana and organized the wild tribes and their lands
to serve Rome.

The Emperor Trajan, who reigned from A.D. 99 to 117,

built 47,000 miles of Roman roads that linked the farthest points of the empire and opened up Europe's interior to exploration and conquest. These roads provided the Romans with efficient land travel that was not equaled again in Europe until the nineteenth century. They were so well engineered that some are still used today.

The first notable observer of nature in the Western world was Aristotle, the Greek philosopher and naturalist who lived more than three centuries before Christ. But the Romans observed the new worlds they conquered with lively curiosity, too. In the first century A.D., Pliny the Elder of Rome compiled his *Naturalis Historia,* a thirty-seven-volume encyclopedia of natural history. An avid and uncritical gatherer of data, Pliny drew not only upon his own experiences in writing this major opus, but also included observations garnered from hundreds of other writers. A few of the subjects covered were the sun, moon, stars, and other heavenly bodies, earthly phenomena, animals, birds, insects, plants, and minerals. Presented uncritically, a great deal of the material was inaccurate; but the *Natural History* also included a number of scientifically sound accounts, most of them taken from Aristotle.

The Roman citizens, however, were able to observe the wild beasts of the empire and the world beyond it in quite direct fashion. In the third century B.C., the consul Metellus exhibited 142 elephants captured at Carthage. Later rulers celebrated their military victories by entertaining the populace with beast baiting—contests setting beast against beast and beasts against men in exhausting life-and-death struggles—as well as with fierce hand-to-hand combats, chariot racing, and gladiator contests staged in large arenas. The Circus Maximus, a mammoth structure 2000 feet long and 600 feet wide and seating 250,000 people, was the largest of these arenas.

In the autumn of 55 B.C., the Roman general and statesman,

Pompey the Great, celebrated one of his many triumphs with the killing of 20 elephants in the Circus Maximus, where he also exhibited 600 lions and 400 other big cats. Not to be out-done, Julius Caesar celebrated his triumph over Pompey, in 46 B.C., in similar fashion and was escorted to and from the Capitol by 40 elephants. For other celebrations, Caesar imported 400 lions to Rome, as well as the first giraffe ever to be seen there. The Emperor Augustus, during his reign from 27 B.C. to A.D. 14, is said to have imported about 3500 animals for the 26 celebrations, or *venationes,* he staged during his rule. These reportedly included 420 tigers, 260 lions, 600 African leopards, cheetahs, and other spotted cats. As though trying to top all of his predecessors, the Emperor Titus brought in 9000 animals in the year A.D. 80 to be killed in a 100-day show at the opening of the Coliseum. The examples could go on and on. But mercifully, the Emperor Constantine issued an edict against such spectacles in the year A.D. 326, and they gradually faded. By this time the Roman Empire was fading as well, and soon the period known as the Dark Ages settled over Europe.

The Dark Ages

After the disintegration of the Roman Empire, Europe sank into an unenlightened period that lasted almost one thousand years, during which time there were few significant advances in science, the arts, or knowledge of any kind. Secure in their cloistered monasteries, monks became the keepers of all wisdom of past ages. Most of the people lived in walled and fortified towns, in small city-states, or under the protection of feudal lords who were always on guard against possible attacks by neighboring rulers. The trade and commerce that had flourished in ancient times with Asia and Africa was greatly curtailed.

Little changed during this period. Northern Scandinavia re-mained as wild as ever, with its frozen taiga and treeless plains inhabited only by hardy, wandering nomads who hunted rein-deer. The vast forests of northern and eastern Europe were the home of the moose, bison, and the wild ox, or aurochs. Shaggy brown bears also roamed the forests, and the howls of wolves could be heard from one end of the continent to the other.

There were no animal shows and circuses as there had been in Roman times but a few medieval towns had bear pits where the people could see a European brown bear or two. Once in a while a traveling showman came to town with a tame dancing bear. Except for these few contacts, most people thought of wild animals only as fierce beasts of the forest—wolves and bears and wildcats—which were to be avoided. Or they were viewed as harmless and tasty game species, such as the rabbit and deer, which were hunted at the risk of punishment from an irate feudal lord who considered them his quarry.

The Renaissance

After almost a thousand years of comparative darkness, sci-ence and the arts began to flourish once again with the coming of the Renaissance. Backward city-states became consolidated, and exploration and commerce expanded in many directions.

In the year 1317, the powerful city-state of Venice, already carrying on a flourishing business with Asia and Africa, opened a galley service with regular trading routes between the Adriatic Sea and northern Europe. "By means of those galleys," observes the historian A. P. Newton, "the ginger of Malabar and the cloves of Ternate, the cinnamon of Ceylon and the nutmegs of Malacca, the camphor of Borneo and the aloes of Socotra, not to mention the chinaware from China found their way into English homes."

European man had not yet conquered the known world, but as a result of the Renaissance he was beginning to make his presence known throughout the Old World. How his expanding trade and civilization affected some of Europe's wildlife is reflected in the following accounts.

WOOLLY MAMMOTH
Elephas primigenius

Some fifteen thousand years ago, a little band of Ice Age hunters gazed happily at the huge beast that stood trapped and helpless before them. Here was a source of abundant food for the entire band. A hairy elephant had stumbled into a natural pit lined with huge boulders and scoured out by glaciers—a deadly hazard for lumbering beasts such as this one. There were many such traps in this area that we now know as France.

Trumpeting with rage, the giant animal struggled to free itself, but succeeded only in wedging its vast bulk more firmly into the crevasse. Nine feet high at the shoulder hump, the mammoth was covered with long shaggy hair. Thick yellowish tusks, each measuring nearly eight feet along its crescent sweep, jutted out on either side of its grasping trunk.

The band of hunters attacked the helpless giant with clubs and spears tipped with sharp stone points. The victim's bellows

echoed and reechoed across the valley as the attack continued. Soon blood streamed from the beast's wounds. Even so, many hours passed before it finally died. Then the primitive hunters hacked it to pieces with their stone knives and axes. Afterward they feasted in celebration; the mammoth's meat would feed the band for many days.

The years went by, and a river of ice buried the bony remains of the mammoth under many feet of glacial till. The giant's bones remained buried for thousands of years while the vast ice sheet ebbed and finally receded.

During excavation for a cathedral in southern France during the late Middle Ages, workmen uncovered the huge bones. These remains were a source of much wonder. Could giant men have lived there before the great flood? Could the great curving tusks be the horns of unicorns? Some men, more learned than others, pointed out that the bones and tusks were very much like those of elephants—those legendary beasts that the ancients were said to have used in war. Could these be the remains of an elephant brought over by the renowned Carthaginian general Hannibal, when he marched on Rome in 218 B.C.? The possibilities were many, but no one knew for certain.

In years to come mammoth bones and tusks were found in other European countries. In 1611, an enterprising Englishman named Josias Logan exhibited in London a mammoth tusk that he had brought from Russia. Other Siberian travelers reported seeing similar beastlike remains in that vast frozen land and also related that both the Siberians and Chinese had for many hundreds of years conducted a flourishing ivory trade with the tusks. The Lapp people of the Far North were said to talk of monstrous beasts that lived under the eternal snows; some Asiatics claimed that the creatures were huge moles that died when they surfaced from under the ground.

In 1692, a Dutch diplomat, Evert Ysbrants Ides, traveled

to China on a mission to the Chinese emperor K'ang-Hsi, on behalf of Russia's ruler, Peter the Great. Upon returning, he reported on the many mammoth remains he found in northern areas he had visited. "But the old Siberian Russians affirm that the *Mammuth* is very like the *Elephant*," he declared. "They also are of the opinion that there were Elephants in this Country before the Deluge, when this climate was warmer, and that their drowned bodies floating on the surface of the water of that Flood, were at last wash'd and forced into Subterranean Cavities: But that after this *Noachian* Deluge, the Air which was before warm was changed to cold, and that these Bones have lain frozen in the Earth ever since, and so are preserved from putrefaction till they thaw, and come to light; which is no very unreasonable conjecture."

In 1799, the eminent zoologist Johann Friedrich Blumenbach stated that, based on the evidence of remains that he had been studying for years in Germany, an elephant had indeed once lived in Europe. It had tusks that curved in a great arc, much more of a curve than the tusks of the living Indian elephant. Blumenbach named this beast *Elephas primigenius*. His conclusions were reinforced by the discovery in 1864 of an Ice Age carving of a mammoth on a piece of ivory at La Madeleine in northern France, as well as later discoveries of mammoth paintings in caves of the Dordogne region of France.

There certainly were no mammoths still living in Europe in the nineteenth century, and scientists speculated that the species had evidently shifted its range to northern Asia when Europe's climate warmed up after the last glacial retreat. Many mammoth remains were found in Siberia, some in remarkable stages of preservation.

In 1901, an almost perfectly preserved mammoth was found in a melting glacier along the banks of the Berezovka River, a tributary of the Kolyma, in Siberia. The remains were taken to the Zoological Museum in St. Petersburg (now Leningrad), where they were studied in detail. The Berezovka mammoth had a thick coat of reddish wool, with long, black guard hairs. Its stomach contents showed that it ate grasses and other tundra vegetation. Blood samples showed that as a species it was closely related to the Indian elephant of today.

No one knows when the last mammoth died, or why. Some believe that the changing climate after the last ice sheet may have caused its extinction. Others believe that primitive man may have hastened its disappearance by overhunting. And a very few diehards believe that the species may still survive today in Siberia's far northern wilderness.

In 1920, an old Russian hunter told a strange story that seemed to support this possibility to the French chargé d'affaires in Vladivostok. As related by Bernard Heuvelmans in his book, *On the Track of Unknown Animals,* the old hunter related how he had followed huge circular tracks in the snow while traveling in northern Siberia: "All of a sudden I saw one of the animals quite clearly, and must admit I really was afraid. It had stopped by some young saplings. It was a huge elephant with big white tusks, very curved; it was a dark chestnut color as far as I could see. It had fairly long hair on the hindquarters, but it seemed shorter on the front. . . ."

A tall tale? Practically every student of the mammoth or of zoology would probably agree that it was.

TARPAN, OR EUROPEAN WILD HORSE
Equus caballus

Our modern horse is a descendant of the Dawn Horse, or *Eohippus,* a small browsing animal that appeared in North America, Europe, and probably Asia as well, during the Eocene epoch, fifty million years ago. About the size of a fox, *Eohippus* had four toes on each front foot and three on each hind foot.

This distant ancestor of the modern horse eventually died out in the Old World, but in North America it flourished and evolved. Through millions of years of natural selection it gradually increased in size, changed in shape and conformation, and reduced the number of functional toes on each foot to just one, which was encased in a hard protective hoof.

During the Upper Pliocene epoch, more than a million years ago, the genus *Equus* evolved in North America. This is the group to which our modern horse as well as the zebras and wild asses belong. Some of these relatively recent horses migrated to Asia at the beginning of the Ice Age. Others spread into South America. Before the beginning of recent times, however, horses had died out in the Americas. But in the Old World *Equus* spread far and wide, reaching Europe and penetrating southeastward to the shores of the Mediterranean and into Africa.

Wild horses were abundant throughout much of Europe during the time of prehistoric man, who hunted them for food. Cro-Magnon painters depicted wild horses on the walls of many European caves. At some point before recorded history, man also captured and tamed wild horses—probably colts only a few days old. Ever since, man has used horses as faithful mounts and beasts of burden. The domestication of the horse may well have taken place on several different continents at roughly the same time.

Some authorities say that all of our breeds of domestic horses today are descended primarily from the wild horses that roamed southern Asia and the Mideast. Egypt and other early civilizations had domestic horses. By the beginning of the Christian era the Romans had refined the horse by selective breeding and were using it extensively as a riding and work animal.

At the same time, nomadic tribes of central Asia were domesticating the shaggy little wild ponies around them. Eventually the Huns would ride their hardy little mounts westward, to invade and conquer much of Europe during the Dark Ages.

The tarpan was the historic wild horse of Europe. It is still debated whether it stemmed from wild stock that had naturally wandered westward from Asia during prehistoric times or descended from horses that had been domesticated by man during prehistoric times and then had returned to the wild. Whatever its origin, the tarpan survived well into the last century.

A small stocky horse with a tan coat and short black mane, the tarpan once ranged in bands throughout the forests and steppes of eastern Europe. In 1768, the German naturalist and explorer Samuel Gmelin collected four specimens in the vicinity of Voronezh, in the Russian Ukraine north of the Crimea. Forty years later another German zoologist, Peter Simon Pallas, reported that the tarpan still ranged over parts of the Russian Steppes and beyond into central Asia. One of the tarpan's last refuges was a royal game park near Bilgoraj, Poland. The band was protected there but declined during the years 1810 to 1820, and one particularly harsh winter all but decimated the herd.

The remaining few were reportedly killed to feed hungry peasants.

By this time the species was on the decline nearly everywhere. Hunted and killed for food by modern as well as by prehistoric man, the tarpan quickly disappeared in Europe. The last recorded specimen, an aged female, died in 1876, in Askaniya Nova, an area of the Ukraine.

Many zoologists claim that the tarpan and the still-surviving Asiatic, or Przewalski's, horse of central Asia may be the same animal or, at most, different races of the same species. Others, among them two enterprising zoomen, brothers Heinz and Lutz Heck, say that the tarpan was a distinct species. The Hecks endeavored to "re-create" the extinct tarpan at the Munich Zoo a few years ago. They did so by selective breeding of the Asian Przewalski's wild horse with domestic horses that exhibited some of the tarpan's characteristics, and then systematically preserving and crossbreeding any specimens that seemed to strengthen these ancient traits. What they eventually produced was an animal that looked very much like the tarpan of old, but was only a reasonable facsimile and not the true animal.

AUROCHS, OR EUROPEAN WILD OX
Bos primigenius

In 58 B.C., Julius Caesar marched north from Rome and into the forests of Gaul to conquer those backward lands and add them to the Roman Empire. Writing of his adventures, he later described a species of wild cattle that he called urus, which lived in the forests of Germany: ". . . an animal somewhat smaller than the elephant, with the appearance, color, and shape of a bull. They are very strong and agile, and attack every man and beast they catch sight of. The natives take great pains to trap them in pits, and then kill them. . . . It is impossible to domesticate or tame the urus, even if it is caught young. The horns are much larger than those of our oxen, and of quite different shape and appearance."

In Caesar's day the urus, or European wild ox, was a widespread species that roamed throughout the forested areas of Europe. Standing about six feet high at the shoulder, the bull was blackish brown and had long, sharp horns that swept out and forward in a broad curve, then flared upward and in. Cows were a lighter brown than the bulls, and calves were a reddish color, evidently somewhat like the young of the American bison. Living in small herds, these wild oxen ventured out of the sheltering woods into open areas during the summer. In the fall they browsed on forest vegetation and munched on acorns and other nuts.

Writing of the animal in his book, *The History of Four-Footed Beasts and Serpents and Insects,* first published in 1607, the seventeenth-century English naturalist Edward Topsell wrote:

"This beast is called by the *Latines, Urus;* by the *Germans, Aurox,* and *Urox,* and *Grosse vesent;* by the *Lituanians, Thur;* the *Scythians, Bubri;* . . ." He also noted that there was some confusion because certain writers mistook the aurochs for the bison, a quite different species of wild cattle.

Emperor Charlemagne is reported to have hunted the aurochs near Aix-la-Chapelle, France, in the ninth century and the Crusaders saw them as they passed through parts of Germany in the eleventh century. By 1400, however, the species had disappeared nearly everywhere except in Poland, a casualty of hunting and the clearing of forests for settlement and agriculture. And in Poland, their last refuge, the numbers of aurochs dwindled, generation after generation. By 1599, there remained a small herd of only twenty-four aurochs living in a royal preserve in the Jaktorovka Forest, some thirty-five miles southwest of Warsaw.

In 1602, just three years later, the herd had dwindled to four individuals. And in 1620—the same year the Pilgrims landed at Plymouth Rock—there was but a single survivor, which lingered on until 1627. Afterward the aurochs was gone forever.

Our domestic cattle in all likelihood were domesticated from the aurochs. The Greeks and peoples of the Mideast had herds of domestic cattle as early as four thousand years ago. And even today there are wild, or feral, cattle in the Camargue region of southern France, and in wilderness areas of Corsica and Spain that resemble the aurochs.

WISENT, OR EUROPEAN BISON
Bison bonasus

Most of us tend to think of the bison—what we call the buffalo—as an exclusively American animal. But Europe has a closely related but distinct species of bison. Paralleling the misfortunes of the American bison, the European species almost became extinct during the nineteenth century, but was saved through the efforts of a few dedicated conservationists.

Quite similar in appearance to the American bison, the wisent is less stocky and has longer legs and a longer tail. Its shoulder hump is less pronounced, and its woolly mane is thinner. More of a browsing than a grazing animal, it travels in small bands and inhabits woodlands.

In ancient times the wisent ranged over most of the forested areas of temperate Europe, eastward to the Caucasus of southeastern Russia. The Romans, busy subduing the stubborn Franks, saw wisent in the wilderness forests of Germany and at various times exhibited them in their amphitheaters. By the time of the Middle Ages, however, a thousand years of hunting, clearing, and settling the land had caused the wisent to disappear over much of Europe.

By 1800 as few as a thousand individuals of the southern, or Caucasian, race still roamed the steppes north of the Black

Sea, and only several hundred of the northern wisent survived in protected forested areas of the Polish-Russian frontier.

One of these areas was the 300,000-acre Bialowieza Forest, a royal hunting preserve—first of the Polish kings, then of the Russian czars. During the Napoleonic Wars, the wisents of Bialowieza dwindled to about 300 animals. By 1857, however, the herd had increased to nearly 2000 in this protected forest refuge. A few years later, in 1865, Czar Alexander II had a bull and three cows from the Bialowieza herd sent to a reserve breeding center in the Pszczyna forest in Upper Silesia. This group had increased to 70 animals by the start of World War I in 1914; at the same time the herd in Bialowieza had decreased to 737 animals.

During the war many German and Russian troops fought in and around Bialowieza, and many of the bison were slaughtered. Following Russia's armistice with the Germans, most of the remaining individuals were killed by marauding peasants and revolutionaries. By 1921, the last wild bison in the preserve had disappeared. The same fate befell the band of wisent in Upper Silesia, with only three individuals preserved in captivity. The last wild survivor of the Caucasian wisent was reportedly killed by a poacher in 1919. A few of them, however, may have survived until 1925. At that time the only remaining wisent in the world were about fifty-five specimens in zoos and in several small private preserves.

Alarmed that the species was about to suffer the same fate as the tarpan and aurochs, zoo men and conservationists met in 1923 at the Berlin Zoo and founded the International Association for the Preservation of the European Bison. They then took immediate steps to protect the remaining stock and kept records so that the pure-blooded individuals (those without any American bison or domestic cattle blood) would be known. The first

Pedigree Book of the European Bison, published in 1930, included data on forty animals. Among them were members of a small herd that the Duke of Bedford, an ardent English naturalist and conservationist, had carefully nurtured on his Woburn Abbey estate in England. By 1933, the herd numbered twenty pure-blooded animals and nineteen that were tainted by a small amount of domestic cattle blood.

In 1929, two survivors of the old Silesian herd were joined with two cows sent by Sweden's Skansen Zoo and a bull from Germany. These five were sent to Bialowieza in a brave attempt to reestablish the wisent in its native habitat. The bison were kept in a fenced enclosure and by 1939, on the eve of World War II, had increased to thirty head. In spite of the hazards of war, this nuclear band survived; six years later, in 1945, they numbered forty-four animals. Twelve additional specimens survived in German zoos and in several other animal collections throughout the world. The European Bison Society, for its part, had kept careful pedigree records, and the blood lines of these individuals were well-documented.

Today, thanks to such careful preservation efforts, there are more than one thousand European bison surviving worldwide, and the number continues to grow larger. Several hundred of them are in the USSR. Pure-blooded animals of the Caucasian wisent are now officially extinct, but a herd of about five hundred with a very small amount of American-bison blood now roams the Caucasus National Park in Russia.

In 1952, the Polish authorities released some of their captive herd in the Bialowieza forest, the site of the centuries-old bison preserve. Today it is believed there are 200 purebred bison there. Most of them roam free within a 10,000-acre Bialowieza National Park, which is enclosed with a head-high fence. Moose, red and roe deer, and about a dozen wolves also roam the area, which is now a tourist attraction.

In 1974, according to the census of rare animals in the *International Zoo Yearbook* for 1975, there were more than 800 wisent held in captive worldwide collections, and approximately 650 in free-ranging herds in Poland and the USSR. With such a pool of both captive and free individuals, the future of the species seems secure.

EUROPEAN IBEX
Capra pyrenaica

Judging from cave paintings, the ibex, with its handsome curved horns, was a common animal in Europe long before the beginning of civilization. Besides painting their likenesses on the walls of caves, prehistoric hunters pursued this fleet-footed wild goat with their crude weapons and sometimes killed them by driving them off cliffs.

When the glaciers retreated, the ibex took refuge on the

craggy slopes and hidden, glacier-filled valleys of the Pyrenees Mountains of France and Spain, and in the Alps of Italy, Switzerland, France, and Austria. There man continued to hunt them. Edward Topsell admired the graceful mountain animals, and remarked: "First these are bred in the Alpes, and are of an admirable celerity, although their heads are loaded with such horns as no other beasts of their stature beareth."

By 1700, the ibex was a rare animal in Europe, seemingly on its way to extinction. The Pyrenean race had once been common, but it diminished swiftly under relentless hunting pressure, and by the twentieth century was almost gone. Today the population of this race may be under twenty animals.

In the Alps the ibex had been killed off by 1850, except for a small remnant population of perhaps sixty animals that survived in the mountainous Piedmont region of northwestern Italy. In 1865, King Victor Emmanuel gave this group a reprieve by protecting the survivors in a royal hunting preserve, the Gran Paradiso. Under protection the population slowly increased. The preserve was upgraded to become Grand Paradiso National Park in 1922, and by 1938 the ibex population in the area had grown to about three thousand head.

After the rigors of World War II, only 419 Alpine ibex could be counted in the region—just one seventh of the prewar population. Under beneficial peacetime conditions, however, the population again built up to about 2500 during the next ten years. And by the early 1960s there were at least 3500 ibex in Italy.

Through the years, many of them have been captured and transplanted to areas within the natural range where they had long since disappeared. Today there are numerous flourishing colonies of Alpine ibex in Switzerland, France, Austria, and Yugoslavia, and the future of the animal looks promising indeed. If similar measures are taken, the Pyrenees ibex may be saved as well.

EUROPEAN WHITE STORK
Ciconia ciconia

Gliding on widespread wings, a large white bird sweeps downward and makes a majestic landing on the rim of its bulky nest on a chimney top. A second bird, a female, sits on the nest. Head thrust back, the female bird welcomes her mate with a rapid, loud clattering of her bill. The male answers in turn, for this behavior is the traditional stork ceremony that marks the changing of the guard at the nest. Greetings over, the female takes off to eat and bathe. The male then settles over the eggs, carefully straddling them by folding his long spindly legs beneath him.

A handsome bird, with snowy white body plumage, gleaming black flight feathers, and red beak and legs, the European white stork is one of the continent's most beloved birds. It has long been considered a symbol of good luck, and the ancient Greeks are said to have believed that a stork nest on the rooftop meant one's aging parents would be protected. The people of Teutonic countries also welcomed the bird as a harbinger of good fortune, and the myth of the stork as the deliverer of babies is a universal one.

The bulky nest—built of sticks and grass and added to yearly—sometimes measures six feet from side to side and may weigh several hundred pounds. Customarily built on a rooftop, chimney, or church clock tower, it can be seen for blocks around.

Returning to Europe each springtime from their wintering grounds in southern climes, white storks quickly set about their annual round of courtship, nest building, egg laying and incubating, and raising young. By July, the two to four young storks are already learning how to fly. Fully fledged in August, the young birds join their parents and other relatives in large flocks, preparatory to migrating south for the winter. The western European stork flyways take them to Spain, then south to Africa as far as the Cape of Good Hope. Central European birds usually travel by way of the Straits of the Dardanelles, skirting the shores of the Mediterranean to the Mideast, and then south to central Africa by way of the Nile.

Stork populations have decreased alarmingly during the past century, especially in central Europe during the last forty years. Denmark, which boasted an estimated 10,000 storks in 1870, reported just 2400 in 1939, 600 in 1949, and a mere 80 birds in 1975. Germany counted 9035 pairs in 1934, but its stork population had dropped to half that number by 1958. Holland had 273 nesting pairs in 1934, but they had dwindled to only 8 pairs in 1974. No native storks have bred in Switzerland since 1949 or in Sweden since 1954.

There are many reasons for this steady rate of attrition. As one stork watcher has stated: "For storks, the modern facts of life are smokestacks, power lines, trains and planes, pesticides and destroyed wetlands." And, as Roger Tory Peterson has observed even more simply: ". . . storks just don't mix with modern cities." Besides the dangers of the breeding season, the birds also run a gauntlet of dangers during the long migration flights to Africa: the hazards of high-tension wires, trigger-happy "sportsmen," pesticide-loaded foods, and poisons placed out to control locusts in Egypt and other African countries.

But in spite of all the obstacles, storks nesting in Europe still total several hundred thousand birds—a great reduction from the years past, but still a good number. Most of them are in Poland and other eastern European countries. Every year stork enthusiasts band nestlings by the thousands in order to keep track of the latest population trends. Platforms are erected on rooftops to encourage nesting, and artificial nests are woven and set up for the birds to adapt to their own purposes. Several successful efforts have been made to bring nestling Algerian storks to Switzerland and other European countries and raise them there. The hope is that these birds, once they have reached maturity and established their natural migratory patterns, will return to nest in the locality where they were raised.

The Status of Other Animals

Compared to Asia or Africa, Europe has a small land mass and a higher human population density per square mile. For thousands of years its land and wildlife have been abused by man in many ways. Much of the land has been stripped of its forests and overcultivated, with consequent erosion, especially in the Mediterranean region. Twenty-five hundred years ago Plato observed that in Greece, "The soft rich soil has been washed away and only the skeleton of the land remains." In the last two centuries the continent has endured the excesses of the Industrial Revolution, with consequent overdevelopment, overpopulation, pollution, and the crowding of too many people into areas too small to support them. The pressures on the land have been acute.

Yet most of Europe's wildlife populations have fared better through the centuries than one might expect. Ironically, as a result of hunting—for centuries a favorite pastime of the European aristocracy—many animal species have been saved from extinction. Because the ruling classes valued a plentiful supply of game to kill, their hunting lands were usually off limits to everyone except royalty. Many game parks and preserves were established on these restricted lands where wildlife was managed and protected from large-scale killing. Consequently, most animals that still existed in Europe in Greek and Roman times survive to some extent even today.

The predatory animals have, of course, suffered the most. Men have always feared and hated them and viewed them as competitors in the hunt. Two thousand years ago lions still roamed southeastern Europe, but the ancient Greeks and their contemporaries exterminated them. The European brown bear, a close relative of the American grizzly, was killed off in England in the eleventh century; it disappeared from Germany during the nineteenth century and from the Swiss Alps by the early twentieth century. A few of these brown bears still maintain a precarious existence in the Pyrenees Mountains of France and Spain, and small remnant populations survive in remote areas of the Far North and the Balkans. But Russia is the only European country that still has brown bears in any appreciable numbers. Man can tolerate such potentially dangerous animals only in isolated, remote areas where they do not conflict with his way of life.

This situation is also that of another predator, the wolf. Hunted and killed everywhere in its range since ancient times, it is a resourceful animal, which still manages to cling to pockets of remote territory where it does not confront its only enemy— man. A few wolves survive in the mountainous forests of Italy, Spain, Poland, Greece, and several of the Balkan countries. But only in the USSR can they still be found in substantial numbers. In some sections of Russia, bounties are offered for slain wolves; in other areas their populations are protected or managed, much as in parts of Canada and the northern United States. Although a half million wolves have been killed in Russia since 1945, wildlife biologists estimated in 1973 that the country still had about 120,000 of them.

Small numbers of the European wildcat still hold on in wild areas, but the rarest predator of them all is probably the Spanish lynx, a subspecies of the European lynx. It is found only in the mountains and delta region of Spain, where there may be as few as fifteen pairs left.

Spanish lynx

Europe's deer, managed and protected as game animals for many centuries, have survived in good numbers. The red deer and the roe deer are managed and hunted much as the American whitetail deer. The European moose had all but disappeared from the forests of Sweden and other Scandinavian countries by the early 1800s. It has recovered well under protection, however, and Sweden now harvests thousands of the animals in annual hunting seasons without affecting the stability of the population.

Russia's northern borders also support a healthy moose population.

The European beaver was nearly eliminated centuries ago, as was its American cousin, because the whims of fashion once dictated beaver hats for men. Beaver fur is not as fashionable today, and as a result the species has recently recovered in many areas. In addition, numerous transplants have been made to reintroduce the beaver to its former range.

The Mediterranean monk seal—the seal known to the ancient Romans and Greeks and featured on Greek coins nearly twenty-five hundred years ago—has been relentlessly killed by fishermen since prehistoric times. Hunted for its handsome pelt, the monk seal is perilously close to extinction, although it still survives in small bands on the coasts of Corsica, Yugoslavia, and Bulgaria as well as on a few islands.

Many of Europe's seabirds are endangered as a result of widespread pollution of every sea in and around Europe, especially the Mediterranean. All of these waters are becoming increasingly befouled with raw sewage, industrial wastes, and pesticides used in agriculture. Many birds of prey are also in trouble because of the buildup of pesticides in the food they eat. The rarest bird in Europe today is probably the Spanish imperial eagle, a large and beautiful bird with white shoulders and a creamy-yellow head. Confined to central and southern Spain— with perhaps a few nonbreeding individuals in northern Morocco and Algeria—this race is thought to number no more than one hundred individuals, including a maximum of thirty adult pairs. In the past, much of the bird's decline could be traced to habitat destruction and to direct killing by man. Today, however, the Spanish imperial eagle is legally protected throughout the Iberian Peninsula and breeds in several refuges and national parks.

European bird lovers are deeply concerned about the problems of pollution and pesticides. They also worry about the widespread and time-honored practice of netting and shooting songbirds in southern Europe—especially Italy—during the fall and spring migrations to and from Africa. According to some estimates, as many as 150 million small birds have been killed annually as a result of such open seasons. In recent years many Save the Birds campaigns have been waged throughout Europe by conservation organizations and concerned citizens, and there has been some success in curbing the shooting and restoring sanctuaries in southern Italy for the migrants. But in many areas the practice continues.

Stretching from the shore of the icy Arctic Ocean to the warm waters of the Indian Ocean, from the Mediterranean to the Pacific, the earth's largest landmass . . . possesses the highest mountains, the vastest deserts, the widest stretches of forests and steppes, the most desolate tundras, the deepest lakes, and several of the longest rivers in the world. Pierre Pfeffer

3

ASIA, THE IMMENSE LAND

Largest of all the continents, Asia encompasses nearly 30 percent of our planet's land and more than half of its human population. Asia stands apart, not only for its vastness, but also because of its endless variety of life forms. Situated at the world's crossroads, Asia is closely linked with all the other continents except South America. Throughout the ages Asia has been a source of plants, animals, and culture to the other continents.

The two most populous nations in the world—China and India—are in Asia. Each of these great countries boasts a civilization and heritage thousands of years old. Since World War II they have been struggling to emerge from centuries of subjugation and exploitation at the hands not only of Western colonial nations but also of invading neighbors and their own

61

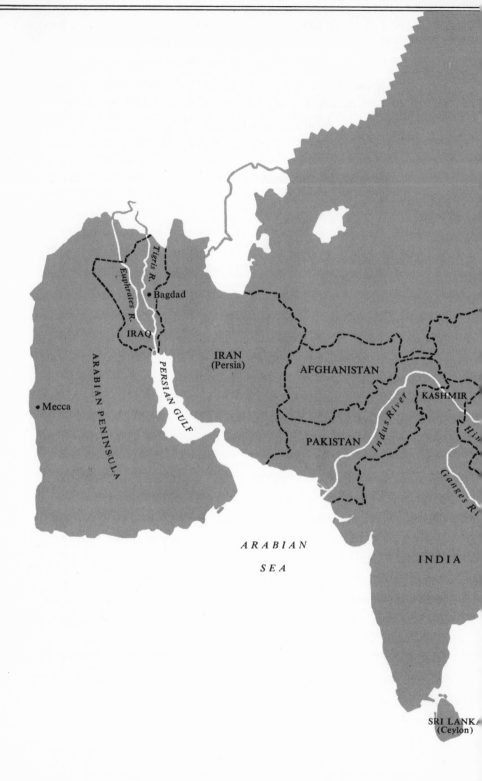

Tigris R.

Euphrates R.

• Bagdad

IRAQ

ARABIAN PENINSULA

• Mecca

PERSIAN GULF

IRAN
(Persia)

AFGHANISTAN

PAKISTAN

Indus River

KASHMIR

Hin

Ganges Ri

ARABIAN

SEA

INDIA

SRI LANKA
(Ceylon)

INDIAN OCEAN

ASIA

SIBERIA

...ON OF SOVIET SOCIALIST REPUBLICS
(Russia)

MONGOLIA

GOBI DESERT

CHINA

Vladivostok

JAPAN

KOREA

Huang River

(Yellow)

Peking

SZECHWAN

PACIFIC OCEAN

TAIWAN

...ins

Brahmaputra R.

BURMA

THAILAND

VIETNAM

SOUTH CHINA SEA

MALAYA

rulers and warlords. Today these two countries have more than one and a quarter billion people between them, and the numbers increase every year. Much of Asia suffers from overcrowding of the human species, especially in the southeast. But other areas of the continent are empty—too inhospitable for man to inhabit.

In Asia's far north lie thousands of miles of frozen tundra, and endless stretches of subarctic taiga—forests of larch, fir, and spruce, intermixed with birch and aspen. Below lie the steppes—great plains and grasslands stretching from China to the Balkan lands of Europe. In prehistoric times the steppes were a gateway to and from Europe for many forms of wildlife; and within the past two thousand years they have served as a highway for Huns and other invading tribes. To the south of the steppes, and around them, are the vast deserts of central and southwestern Asia—burning hot in summer and freezing cold in winter—and below range the awesome, snow-covered peaks of the Himalayas. To the south and west of these mountains lie the temperate forest lands and the rice bowls of China, as well as the steaming, tropical rain forests of India, Indochina, and Malaya.

With hundreds of soaring snow-covered peaks, higher than any other mountains in the world, the Himalayas forge a craggy barrier, an almost insuperable dividing line between the zoogeographic region known as the Palaearctic realm to the north, and the mostly tropical Oriental realm of southeastern Asia. All in all, the continent forms a vast treasure-house of human history and of countless living things as well.

Early Asiatic Civilizations

Western civilization rose along the shores of the Mediterranean and reached its highest accomplishments in Europe. But while this smaller continent was still largely wilderness, with a few tribes just beginning to emerge from barbarism, Asia was already the homeland of many complex and highly sophisticated civilizations.

In the Bible lands of the Near East—especially in that fertile spot between the Tigris and Euphrates Rivers that used to be called Mesopotamia and is now in the modern state of Iraq— a bewildering succession of dynasties and kingdoms had already come and gone. For good reason this area has been called the Cradle of Civilization. Among the first advanced peoples in this area were the Sumerians, who developed a sophisticated civilization as early as 3500 B.C. Building on the Sumerian foundation, the Babylonians advanced the practice of agriculture, irrigation, and animal husbandry, and they further developed arts and architecture. Under King Hammurabi, a complex code of laws was worked out about 2000 B.C. Many other groups rose to temporary power in this region and vied with one another for power. Among them were the Hittites, Assyrians, Chaldeans, and Persians.

Persia reached its summit of power under King Cyrus and his immediate followers about 500 B.C. Under their vigorous military leadership, Persia conquered Egypt and most of the Near East and ruled an empire that stretched from Egypt to India. Less than two hundred years later, however, the Greeks challenged Persian dominance and marched toward India under Alexander the Great.

India was the meeting ground where many different peoples —Aryans, Mongols, Huns, and countless primitive tribes—met and mixed over thousands of years of invasion, migration, and assimilation. By the time of Alexander, the great southern peninsula boasted a number of highly developed civilizations. All of the world's principal religions—Hinduism, Buddhism, Islam, and Christianity (each of them Asiatic in origin)—finally met in India, a meeting place of travelers and merchants from all points of the compass. The influence of these religions spread both east and west. In the same way, the civilizations and peoples of India influenced all the other Asiatic countries around them, especially those of southeastern Asia and the islands of the Malay Archipelago.

China, that vast land to the north and east of India, has had an equally ancient and advanced civilization. When the philosopher Confucius wrote his maxims for life's conduct, about 500 B.C., China already had a long, respected history known as the Middle Kingdom with its cultivated arts and sciences.

Ancient Trade Routes Between Europe and Asia

Trade and commerce had flourished between the Mediterranean and the lands of southern Asia long before written history. Ancient caravan routes wound their way through high mountain passes and across the steppes and deserts, bringing silks and spices and other produce of the East to the civilizations of the Mideast and southern Europe, in exchange for their timber, ivory and gold from Africa, and the purple dye and fabrics for which the Phoenicians were famous. Sea routes were also used in this commerce, for the Arabs had from earliest times sailed under the monsoon winds from the Red Sea to India. From these ancient mariners, the Phoenicians and others also learned the favored sea routes to southern Asia.

With the rise of the Greeks, new ties with Asia were made through the conquests of their armies. Several centuries later the Romans became dominant in the Mediterranean, and Europe's commerce with Asia further increased. Silk from distant China was highly prized by the luxury-loving Romans, and they spared no efforts in obtaining it. The Chinese kept the source and production of this beautiful fabric a well-guarded secret until the sixth century A.D. In the year 536, however, during the reign of the Roman Emperor Justinian, two monks serving as missionaries in China smuggled silkworm eggs back to Europe in hollow bamboo staffs. With this introduction, the production of silk finally began in Europe.

The intermingling of Eastern and Western cultures increased with the rise of Islam—the fervent and expansionist religious movement of the Moslems in the seventh century A.D. Mohammed the Prophet was born in 570 in Mecca, an Arab city near the shores of the Red Sea. He died in A.D. 632, but his followers swiftly spread his religion and influence far and wide —westward to Morocco and eventually Spain, and eastward to China and the exotic Spice Islands of the far Pacific. During this time, Rome collapsed; the Western world broke up into many splintered parts as Europe descended into the time known as the Dark Ages.

Led by Genghis Khan, the Mongols of northern Asia invaded Europe in 1236, sweeping across Russia with their fierce cavalry, devastating Poland and Hungary, and dominating these east-European lands for some two hundred years. The Mongol horsemen swept over the Mideast as well, capturing Baghdad in 1258. Two years later Kublai Khan, the grandson of Genghis Khan, was elected the Great Khan of the Chinese empire.

At this time Marco Polo, Venetian merchant, traveled with his father to the Great Khan's court and there entered his service for over twenty years—from 1271 until his return to Venice in 1295.

The Travels of Marco Polo

"Polo was the first traveller to trace a route across the whole longitude of Asia," one biographer says, "describing kingdoms which he had seen; the first to speak of the court at Peking; the first to reveal China in its wealth and vastness, and to tell of the nations on its borders."

Three years after his return to Venice in 1295, Marco Polo

was taken prisoner by the forces of Genoa in one of the many military struggles between Venice and her rival city-states. He languished in prison for a year, and while there dictated his Asiatic adventures to a fellow prisoner. Forever after, *The Book of Marco Polo* linked the knowledge of East and West.

His detailed descriptions were colorful and generally accurate. He gave many vivid word pictures of the life of the people and their relationship to the animals around them. "The emperor has numbers of leopards trained to the chase," he wrote, "and has also a great many lynxes taught in like manner to catch game, and which afford excellent sport. He also has several great lions, bigger than those of Babylonia, beasts whose skins are colored in the most beautiful way, being striped all along the sides with black, red, and white."

When the emperor went on a hunting expedition, Marco Polo noted, "He takes with him full ten thousand falconers, and some five hundred gerfalcons besides peregrines, sakers, and other hawks in great numbers; and goshawks also to fly at the waterfowl." He further described what must have been one of the earliest kinds of game management and protection. ". . . throughout all the emperor's territories, nobody however audacious dares to hunt any of these four animals, to wit, hare, stag, buck, and roe, from the month of March to the month of October. . . . And thus the game multiplies at such a rate that the whole country swarms with it. . . . Beyond the term I have mentioned, however, to wit, that from March to October, everybody may take these animals as he list."

Marco Polo pointed the way, but another two centuries were to pass before the modern era of Western exploration and exploitation of Asia and the fabled Spice Islands would really begin. Only then did the complex variety of the land and wildlife of Asia gradually begin to be more completely known.

ASIATIC ELEPHANT
Elephas maximus

Native to India and southeastern Asia, the Asiatic elephant in appearance looks like a throwback to the mammoths of the Ice Age. Indeed, it and its African relative are the only two surviving members of a huge and diverse group that once included many species that wandered over all the world, except Australia. Both the Asiatic and African elephants have been domesticated by man, but the Asiatic species has been used to a far greater extent.

Weighing up to six tons, and with a shoulder height of nine feet or more, the Asiatic elephant has incredible strength and endurance. Possessing a high level of intelligence, it has been man's servant and companion for thousands of years and is useful in many different roles: as an efficient beast of burden, as a hunting platform, as a bulldozer in road building or a carrier of logs in forestry operations, as a performer in religious ceremonies and circuses, and as a tank or battering ram during wartime.

The use of elephants in battle goes back thousands of years. When Alexander the Great campaigned in Asia, Darius of Persia opposed him in 331 B.C. with fifteen elephants supporting his armies of men. The Persian forces were routed, however, and the elephants captured. Later described by Aristotle, they became part of recorded history.

Just five years later, at the Battle of Jhelum, the Indian King Dorus opposed Alexander's advance with "200 elephants like walking ramparts in the center of his army, with archers in the wings." Once again, the Asian forces were defeated after a hard battle. But the account shows that Asian rulers of the period had long been accustomed to using elephants in warfare.

Elephants were well-known in Rome and its provinces during the flowering of the Roman Empire, for they were featured in many spectacles and circuses at the arenas and the Circus Maximus. Ever since those days, elephants have been popular animals in zoos and circuses all over the world.

There were several traditional ways of capturing wild elephants for domestication. One method was to construct a pit, cushioned at the bottom with branches and leaves and camouflaged with leafy branches across the top. After falling in, the elephant was trapped. A sloping ramp was then dug down into the pit and the shackled victim led out, usually escorted by a tame elephant. Another method of capture was the use of a noose that snared the beast by the leg.

The most famous method, however, was the capture of an entire herd of elephants at one time in a huge and stoutly built stockade known as a *khedda*. The *khedda* had a comparatively narrow opening, from which long extensions of the wall flared wider and wider outward, forming a funnel. Trained men called beaters would surround a group of wild elephants and herd them toward the *khedda* by beating on drums and making loud noises. Hurrying through the arms of the stockade, the frightened animals were funnelled through the narrow opening. The heavy gates were then closed, and the elephants trapped. Reliable tame elephants were used to separate and calm the wild captives.

Before 1945 the *khedda* was the prevalent method used for capturing elephants in British colonial India. As recently as 1968, elephants were captured by this method in the Indian state of Mysore. The elephant roundup that year may have been the last, however, for a projected dam on the Kabbani River will flood the best elephant habitat. Besides, the use of domestic elephants in India has declined sharply in recent years.

This decrease began after World War I, when cars and trucks were introduced into India and Burma. The trend away from elephants was even more marked after World War II, when India gained her independence from Britain and much wild country began to be opened up for agriculture and forestry activities. Many of the forests, which had for centuries provided food and sanctuary for elephants, were cleared for crops and destroyed in extensive lumbering operations. And instead of preserving diverse natural forests by reseeding, uniform stands of such exotic trees as eucalyptus were planted in many areas for the paper-pulp industry. Such uniform tree farms provide poor eating for elephants.

As a result of this destruction of habitat and food, elephant populations have declined steadily. Once the pride of India, the elephant has now been relegated to the status of unwanted animal in many areas. "Today," as one elephant expert states, "the only trade that seems to prosper is that which takes the Indian elephants to the zoos and circuses of the world."

Throughout their natural range, the numbers of wild Asiatic elephants continue to shrink annually. From an estimated hundreds of thousands a century ago, the elephant population has dwindled today to perhaps 15,000 to 20,000 in all of Asia.

These animals survive in isolated bands in scattered pockets of their old range. There may be 8000 in India, 500 in Thailand, less than 500 in west Malaysia, 2000 in Borneo, 1500 in Sumatra, and perhaps 3000 in Sri Lanka—once the island kingdom of Ceylon. There are no estimates for Nepal, Burma, or Indochina.

The problems elephants face in Sri Lanka illustrate the problems they are facing everywhere. As early as 1831, the island instituted a bounty system to reduce its elephant herds, for already there were too many beasts for the size of the country and its expanding human population. Close to 10,000 elephants were shot on Ceylon during the nineteenth century. By 1953, fewer than 5000 remained. A few years later, a study and survey of the island's elephants, undertaken between 1966 and 1969 by the Smithsonian Institution and the World Wildlife Fund, indicated a population of just 1500. The Wildlife Department of Sri Lanka disagreed, saying that at least 5000 elephants remained. Most of the survivors, whatever their numbers, are concentrated in the Yala, Wilpattu, and Kumana national reserves.

Today these wild elephants—except for dangerous rogues— are legally protected. But their jungle habitat is fast disappearing. Domestic elephants in the island nation number only about five hundred. Eventually the Sinhalese may breed their tame elephants on a wider scale, but a long-held belief that breeding in captivity ruins an elephant for work still prevails.

The wild elephant's future everywhere depends on the establishment of a number of large reserves that can provide the herds with all the sanctuary and food they need.

PÈRE DAVID'S DEER
Elaphurus davidianus

Abbé Armand David, the noted French naturalist and missionary, was born in 1826 in the little French town of Espelette on the River Nive. From earliest boyhood he was an enthusiastic observer of nature and possessed a keen eye, a lively curiosity, and a sense of wonder. As a young man he took the vows of priesthood and in 1861 went to China as a missionary and naturalist. There Père David set up and directed a school for boys in Peking, but he also spent a great deal of his time exploring the Chinese countryside, taking detailed notes on the plants and animals that he observed and gathering specimens to send back to Europe. Birds were his main interest, but he also studied and collected insects, plants, reptiles, fish, and mammals. In 1865, he made a notable discovery—a new species of deer—as he described in a letter written on September 21 to his friend, Henri Milne-Edwards, a well-known zoologist, who was then director of the Museum of Natural History in Paris.

"A mile from Peking lies the vast Imperial Park, which may be a dozen miles around. . . . No European can go into the Park, but this last spring, climbing on the wall, I was lucky enough to see, although rather far away, a herd of over 100 of these animals which looked to me like moose. Unfortunately they had no antlers at that time. What characterizes the animals I saw was the length of the tail which was proportionately as long as a donkey's. . . . The Chinese gave this animal the name of Mi-lou, and more often that of Ssu-pu-hsiang, which means 'The four characters which do not fit together,' because they find that this reindeer belongs to the stag by his antlers, to the cow by its feet, the camel by its neck, and the mule by its tail."

In his journal, Père David later noted that, although there was reported to be a death penalty for anyone who killed one of these animals in the Imperial Park, the soldiers who supposedly guarded the animals sometimes secretly killed them for food. In 1866, however, the resourceful Père David managed to obtain two skins of the deer—perhaps by bribing the guards —and sent them to his friend, Milne-Edwards. The French zoologist thereupon described the animal and gave it the scientific name, *Elaphurus davidianus,* in honor of the priest-naturalist who had sent the specimens to him.

Two living Père David's deer reached the London Zoo in 1869, through the efforts of Père David and the British minister at Peking. During the next few years others were sent to zoos in Paris, Berlin, and, once again, London. Père David, the discoverer of the species, considered that it had long since been killed off in the wild and had been preserved only by being protected in captivity, perhaps for hundreds of years, in the royal preserve. As later determined by the discovery of fossil remains, the original range of Père David's deer evidently included considerable portions of East Asia—mostly low flatlands along the Yellow River and other waterways from Peking to Shanghai.

The most notable feature of this deer is its unusual set of antlers, quite different from those of any other species. These antlers divide into two main branches, and the forward branch then forks again. Along the nape of the neck there is a skimpy mane of black hair. In winter the animal's coat is dull brown; in spring and summer, it is a warm reddish color. During the mating season, large glands below the eyes of the stag are very noticeable. The rutting stag often becomes quite ill-tempered, digging in the mud with his antlers and bellowing with a hoarse, penetrating grunt. At this time he may on occasion charge any man or animal nearby.

After having survived in the protected enclosure of the Imperial Park near Peking for so long, Père David's deer suffered a major setback at the close of the nineteenth century. Floodwaters of the Hun Ho River breached the walls of the park, and many of the deer drowned or escaped only to be killed for food by hungry peasants. As few as thirty survived. Most of them were subsequently killed in 1900 during the Boxer Rebellion, when European soldiers broke into the park and slaughtered the deer for venison. Only two surviving animals could be counted at Peking in 1911. Ten years later there were none.

Fortunately, there were still some surviving specimens in Europe, descendants of those sent from China years before. Those in zoos had usually been kept by pairs or as individual specimens in small enclosures, and most of them had failed to breed. But the Duke of Bedford, the enthusiastic and determined English naturalist, purchased zoo specimens of Père David's deer wherever and whenever he could. By the turn of the century he had assembled a small herd, which he kept on this 4000-acre ancestral estate at Woburn Abbey.

Conditions there were very much as they had been at the Imperial Hunting Park in China, and the deer prospered. By 1914 the duke's herd had increased to about ninety specimens. After the hard years of World War I, however, these animals had dwindled to about fifty animals. In 1921, they were the only Père David's deer left in the world, for all of the specimens in China and in European zoos had died.

Happily, the Duke of Bedford's herd flourished during the 1920s and 1930s. After World War II, the duke decided that all the specimens should not be kept in one place, in case disease or other disaster should strike. He sent some to Whipsnade, the large animal park operated by the Zoological Society of London. In December, 1946, two bucks and two does were also sent to the New York Zoological Society's Bronx Zoo—the first Père David's deer ever seen in the New World. A fawn was born in New York in 1949, two others in 1951, and thereafter the little band of Père David's deer in the Bronx Zoo increased.

A number of other zoos have since received breeding stock as well, and, in 1956, four specimens were sent from England to China—the land from which they had come in the first place —and installed in the zoological park in Peking. By 1974 the population of Père David's deer had increased to about seven hundred deer, held in some seventy zoos and game parks throughout the world.

The future of Père David's deer in captivity now seems assured. The species is an outstanding example of an animal that was exterminated in the wild but successfully preserved for many hundreds of years in captivity. It is hoped that some of this captive stock may eventually be released in carefully chosen wild preserves in the animal's natural habitat in China. Then Père David's deer can once again be counted as a wild species that has survived—both in spite of man and *because* of man.

PERSIAN FALLOW DEER
Dama mesopotamica

The common European fallow deer (*Dama dama*) is a stocky little species that formerly ranged the shores of the Mediterranean from Spain to the Mideast, and it is said to have been introduced into Britain by the conquering Romans, some two thousand years ago. Today it is widely known as a semitame deer of parks and game reserves, where it often appears in three distinct color phases. Most common is a light fawn color, with many white spots. In addition, there is a white or albino form, and one that is quite dark—sometimes almost black.

A related but quite distinct species is the Persian fallow deer. It differs from the common fallow deer in being somewhat larger, having a brighter reddish-brown coat, with white spots merging into a light line on either side of the black line down the midback, and antlers that are not flattened terminally, as are those of the common fallow deer.

This attractive species once ranged over large areas of the Mideast, from Southern Persia to Jordan and Israel. It has long since disappeared from most of this area, a victim of man's hunting and his encroachment upon the deer's river-bottom habitat for agriculture and the grazing of domestic stock, especially goats. By the late 1960s the population of the Persian fallow deer had dwindled to perhaps two or three dozen individuals, most of them confined to small lowland thickets along the Dez and Karkheh Rivers in southwestern Iran.

The Iranian Government has set up two reserves for the surviving population and has also taken steps to establish a captive breeding herd. Today the deer's numbers are increasing very slowly.

MUSK DEER
Moschus moschiferus

Another endangered species is the little musk deer that ranges through the mountains of central and eastern Asia, from northern India to China, a small antlerless deer with long canine teeth. This species has long been prized for its musk gland, as noted by Marco Polo: "There exists in that region a kind of wild animal like a gazelle. It has feet and tail like the gazelle's, and stag's hair of a very coarse kind, but no horns. It has four tusks, two below and two above, about three inches long, and slender

in form, one pair growing upwards and the other downwards.
. . . When the creature has been taken, they find at the navel
between the flesh and the skin something like an impostume full
of blood, which they cut out and remove with all the skin attached to it. And the blood inside this impostume is the musk
that produces that powerful perfume. . . ."

Today, hundreds of years later, the musk deer is still being
eagerly killed for the abdominal musk gland that is found only
in the male. The species is nominally protected in most areas,
but that does not deter poachers. After a musk deer is trapped
or shot, the gland is removed from the male victim and dried.
Then it is smuggled to Eastern markets where it is utilized in
the concoction of Oriental medicines and as a fixative in the
perfume industry. Up until 1972, an estimated fifteen thousand
to thirty thousand musk deer were killed annually in India alone
for such export. After India's Wildlife Protection Act gave the
species nominal protection that year, the price of each illegally
taken musk pod was quoted as high as 5000 rupees (about $575
dollars at today's rate of exchange).

Today the populations of Asia's musk deer are dwindling
nearly everywhere, and the future of this exploited species is
uncertain.

GIANT PANDA
Ailuropoda melanoleuca

Traveling through western Szechwan Province in 1869,
Père David wrote in his journal for March 23: "My Christian
hunters return today after a ten-day absence. They bring me a
young white bear, which they took alive, but unfortunately killed
so it could be carried more easily. The young white bear, which
they sell to me very dearly, is all white except for the legs, ears,
and around the eyes, which are deep black. . . . This must be

a new species of *Ursus*, very remarkable not only because of its color, but also for its paws, which are hairy underneath, and for other characters."

Within the next two weeks, the hunters brought him other specimens. They knew the giant panda as *hua-hsiung*, "spectacled bear," or sometimes as *pei-hsiung*, "white bear."

Today the rare and beautiful giant panda is used as the symbol of the World Wildlife Fund. Judging from fossil remains, ancestors of the giant panda ranged widely over southern China during the Ice Age. Today, however, the main population is apparently confined to an area less than two hundred miles from north to south in the remote mountain country of central and northern Szechwan Province.

Usually living at altitudes of six to ten thousand feet on rugged mountain slopes covered with mixed forests and thick stands of bamboo, the giant panda apparently feeds almost entirely on the leaves and shoots of the latter. Each of its front paws is equipped with an unusual small pad, which assists the

panda in grasping stalks of bamboo and pulling them down to
its powerful grinding teeth. When it is feeding, the panda may
wander in a zigzag pattern over a mountain slope, stopping at
one bamboo thicket after another. Sometimes it even climbs
trees. It sleeps in nests under ledges or at the base of trees, and
it is believed not to hibernate during the winter.

Ever since Père David brought the species to the attention of
the Western world, scientists have disagreed about whether it is
more closely related to the bear or the raccoon family, or whether
it is perhaps in a family of its own. The giant panda certainly
looks more like a bear than anything else; but its little cousin,
the reddish-colored lesser panda, is decidely raccoonlike.

Although the panda skins collected by Père David were sent
to Europe, the first recorded specimen shot by Westerners was
taken in 1929 by Theodore and Kermit Roosevelt, the adventuresome sons of President Theodore Roosevelt. This specimen was
placed in the Chicago Field Museum of Natural History, where
it still may be seen. In 1934, five years later, an expedition sponsored by the American Museum of Natural History in New
York brought back the skin of an adult female panda that had
been collected in Szechwan.

Mrs. Ruth Harkness, however, was the one who brought
the first living panda to the Western world. In 1935, the New
York Zoological Society had talked with her husband, W. H.
Harkness, about capturing a live panda for the Bronx Zoo collections. Shortly after beginning his quest for a specimen,
Harkness died in Shanghai in February, 1936, before he could
reach panda country. Mrs. Harkness, who had accompanied her
husband, carried on the search in his place. Aided by Quentin
Young, an experienced animal collector, she finally succeeded
on the ninth of November, as she later recorded: "From the old
dead trunk of the tree came a baby's whimper. Quentin reached
into the hollow trunk of the tree. Then he turned and walked

toward me. In his arms was a baby panda." Weighing two and a half pounds, eyes still closed, and probably no more than two weeks old, the baby thrived under Mrs. Harkness's care. Thought to be a female (later found to be a male), the cub was named Su-Lin and ended up in Chicago's Brookfield Zoo—the first giant panda ever seen in captivity.

In quick succession during the next five years, eleven other pandas were brought out of China and delivered to Western zoos. The last two that came out before World War II were Pan-dah and Pan-dee, acquired by the New York Zoological Society in December, 1941. The war and the upheaval in China stopped all panda exports for some years—and probably just as well.

Various Chinese zoos secured pandas for their collections, however, and in 1963 the Peking Zoo exhibited the first panda cub bred and born in captivity. Several other zoo births have occurred since at both this zoo and the Shanghai Zoo. The Chinese are very proud of their unique black-and-white bear and have extended complete protection to it in the wild. No one knows how many there may be, but with such a restricted range there certainly cannot be a great number.

In 1972, China sent a gift of two young pandas, Ling-Ling and Hsing-Hsing, to the United States in exchange for a pair of musk oxen. The only giant pandas in the United States, they are in the National Zoological Park in Washington, D. C.

SNUB-NOSED, OR GOLDEN, MONKEY
Rhinopithecus roxellanae

Traveling through Szechwan Province of China in the spring of 1869—the same spring that he discovered the giant panda— Père David added a new monkey to his list of discovered species. Writing in his journal for the fourth of May, he records: "My hunters, who left a fortnight ago for the eastern regions, return today and bring me six monkeys of a new species which the

Chinese call *chin-tsin-hou,* or golden-brown monkey. These animals are very robust and have large muscular limbs. Their faces are very strange, green-blue or turquoise with the nose turned up almost to the forehead. Their tails are long and strong. Their backs are covered with long hair and they live in trees in the highest mountains, now white with snow."

Specimens were sent back to Europe, where the species was given its scientific name, inspired by Roxellane, a favorite wife of the sixteenth-century Turkish ruler, Suleiman the Magnificent, who was famous for her beauty and upturned nose.

The northernmost representative of the leaf-eating monkeys, the golden monkey, is found in forested mountain country of western China and eastern Tibet. It travels in troops that range through the treetops searching for leaves and fruit to eat. It has long been killed for its handsome pelt, which was reportedly prized as a preventative against rheumatism. Cloaks made from the long, golden fur were reserved to be worn by mandarins.

Never common, the species has been hunted relentlessly for centuries. Today it is legally protected but very rare.

SAIGA ANTELOPE
Saiga tatarica

A stocky, short-legged antelope, the saiga is distinguished by its curiously swollen nasal chambers and downward-curving nostrils. These adaptations may prove useful in moistening and warming the dusty, dry air breathed by the saiga in the areas in which it lives. Besides the inflated nose, the male saiga antelope is equipped with foot-long, slightly curving horns. The story of this species illustrates graphically how an endangered animal can make a dramatic comeback under protective management.

Traveling in herds, the saiga historically ranged across the steppes of Europe and central Asia. It was hunted enthusiastically by the Tartars, Mongols, and other Asiatic tribes, and for hundreds of years the exported horns formed the basis of a flourishing trade with China. The Chinese ground up the horn, which was then used as an aphrodisiac.

The slaughter of the saiga for its horns, and for its meat and hides as well, reached its peak in the middle of the nineteenth century—about the same time as the mass slaughter of the Amer-

ican bison. Sometimes entire herds of saiga antelopes numbering hundreds or thousands were driven into fenced corrals, then killed en masse. By the early years of the twentieth century only scattered remnants of the once-huge bands were left, possibly no more than a thousand antelope in all.

After the overthrow of the czarist government in Russia, the revolutionaries passed a decree in 1919 forbidding the hunting of the endangered saiga. During the next twenty years field biologists conducted detailed observations of the species in the wild, learning its habits and requirements. The animal, they noted, was responding dramatically to protection.

By 1950 the saiga population in Kazakhstan, Russian Asia, had ballooned to an estimated three quarters of a million animals, by 1960 to one and a quarter million. An additional half million roamed the steppes of European Russia west of the Volga River. Today the total population is estimated at more than two million animals, and a controlled annual hunting season allows the harvest of up to a half million animals yearly without causing a decline in the overall population.

"This management on a sustained yield basis," declares Harry A. Goodwin, formerly of the Office of Endangered Species, United States Fish and Wildlife Service, "could be applied to many wildlife species to save them." The concept is certainly applicable to various species of Asiatic deer and other hoofed animals.

ARABIAN ORYX
Oryx leucoryx

Spreading out in a vast skirmish line miles wide, the jeeps and trucks swept over the Arabian deserts, fanning out to inspect every blazing hill and dune—a search-and-destroy operation leveled against every living thing. Ostriches were mowed down with repeating shotguns or high-powered rifles, gazelles and

other antelopes were pursued relentlessly until they either were
felled by rifle shots or dropped from exhaustion. Then the hunters
cut their throats. "Oil companies, soldiers, and local citizens
have all joined the slaughter," remarked one observer in 1963.

As a direct result of these senseless raids, the once-abundant
wildlife of the Arabian Peninsula was decimated and much of
it wiped out in the years following World War II. The beautiful
little Arabian gazelle was reduced from flourishing herds to the
status of an endangered species. The Arabian ostrich almost
vanished. So did the animal that Arab sheiks considered the
greatest prize of all—the beautiful Arabian oryx.

Smallest of the oryx antelopes, the Arabian species stands
little more than three feet high at the shoulder. Its markings are
pale creamy white, with black markings on the face and deep
chocolate on the legs. The long, slender horns are almost straight
and measure up to twenty-nine inches long. Able to live in
desert areas and go for long periods without water, the species
once ranged over most of the Arabian Peninsula, as well as over
the Sinai, lower Palestine, Transjordan, and Iraq.

The animal was a highly prized trophy of past hunts, for the Arabs believed that whoever killed an oryx and ate its flesh would be endowed with its bravery, strength, and endurance. Hunters of the desert tribes pursued it on camelback, pitting their own skill and endurance against their quarry. The oryx could stand such hunting, but when hunters began to pursue the species in motor cars and slaughter them with modern weapons —sometimes even using planes and helicopters for spotting— its numbers began to decrease dramatically.

Lee Talbot, an ecologist with the Smithsonian Institution, tells how, in 1955, some 482 cars took part in such a hunt, during the course of a "royal good-will tour" through northern Arabia, in which the participants shot everything in sight. Little wonder that by 1960 the oryx was almost wiped out, with an estimated population of only one hundred animals or fewer in southern Arabia. Talbot concluded that the only way the species could be saved from extermination would be to capture some specimens and transfer them to a protected habitat.

In 1962, the Fauna Preservation Society and the Survival Service Commission of the Union for the Conservation of Nature and Natural Resources (IUCN) mounted Operation Oryx, aimed at capturing a few oryx for the purpose of establishing a captive breeding herd. Major Ian Grimwood, former Chief Game Warden of Kenya, led the expedition, which succeeded in capturing four oryx in eastern Aden. One of them subsequently died as a result of an old gunshot wound, but the others survived. After quarantine they were shipped to Phoenix, Arizona, where special quarters had been prepared for them at the Phoenix Zoo. Sheik Jabir Abdullah Sabah, the Sultan of Kuwait, donated a fourth oryx to this nucleus, and the London Zoo, a fifth. The oryx thrived in the warm, dry climate of Arizona, and in October, 1963, the first oryx calf was born to this official World Herd. That same year the World Wildlife Fund sponsored a second expedition to capture several more specimens for the herd, but the expedition was unable to find even one wild oryx. Kind Ibn Saud, ruler of Saudi Arabia, donated four additional specimens from his own private game farm, so by the end of 1963 the World Herd had increased to twelve.

Many wildlife experts consider the Arabian oryx extinct in the wild. Others believe that a few may inhabit remote sections of Oman or Aden where roads and civilization have not yet intruded. The survival of the species depends on captive animals, at least until sanctuaries can be set up and protection given to specimens freed in their native habitat. Without captive herds, the oryx would most likely be extinct today.

By 1974 the World Herd totaled sixty-six specimens, all but six of them born in captivity; there were thirty-one in Phoenix, sixteen in Los Angeles, and seven in San Diego. In addition, there were about thirty in the sultan's private herd at Slamy, along the Persian Gulf in northeast Qatar; seven specimens in the breeding herd on the royal game farm at Riyadh, Saudi Arabia; and five captive specimens at Abu Dhabi. Conservationists hope that the day will come when there is peace in the Mideast and some of these captive Arabian oryx can be freed in suitable areas of their native lands.

PRZEWALSKI'S WILD HORSE
Equus przewalskii

Exploring central Asia during the 1870s, a Russian naturalist, Nikolai Mikhailovitch Przewalski, collected many animal specimens for scientific study as well as a great deal of information about the wildlife of the region. He was especially intrigued by a unique wild horse—an animal quite different from the mounts of the nomadic Mongol tribesmen. These wild horses were small and stocky, with an erect black mane but no forelock. With big heads and short legs, they were generally yellowish brown in color, with a light belly and a dark streak down the back. They looked very much like the cave drawings of Europe's Ice Age horse, the long-extinct tarpan.

When he returned to Europe, Przewalski brought back with him a skin and skull of this wild horse he had found. In 1881, I. S. Poliakov, a Russian zoologist, wrote the first scientific description of the animal, naming it after its discoverer.

A few foals were subsequently captured, and in 1900 three living specimens were kept on a Russian estate. At this time the Duke of Bedford, the English animal enthusiast, commissioned Carl Hagenback of Hamburg, Germany, to capture six specimens of Przewalski's horse for his collections at Woburn Abbey. The most noted animal collector of his time, Hagenback had a worldwide network of agents and collectors. He promptly sent agent William Grieger to the Gobi Desert to organize the capture. There, with the aid of nearly two thousand Kirghiz horsemen to run down foals and pregnant mares, Grieger succeeded in capturing fifty-two Przewalski's horses. Of them, twenty-eight survived to be transported to Europe in the fall of 1901. From this nucleus have come practically all of the captive stock of Przewalski's horses alive today.

The species once ranged over much of southwest Mongolia

and parts of the Gobi Desert. Traveling in bands, the little wild horses summered on the high, dry plains and wintered on the southern slopes of the mountains or in protected valleys. They competed for food and water with the domestic stock of nomadic tribesmen, and at times there may have been hybridization with Mongol ponies. The wild population decreased steadily. By the 1940s it had almost disappeared, and by the 1950s Przewalski's horse was considered extinct in the wild.

There have been a few subsequent sightings, however, and possibly a handful may still roam free. Although nominally protected, the only hope for their survival is the establishment of a native preserve from which all domestic stock are excluded.

The survival of the species so far has been assured by the descendants of the animals collected by William Grieger at the turn of the century. In 1974 there were 219 Przewalski's horses in fifty-five zoos or other animal collections around the world. Thirty foals were born in captivity that year. A stud book containing a careful record of all these captive specimens is kept at the Prague Zoo in Czechoslovakia.

Captive animals such as these are no substitute for wild populations. They may serve, however, as seed stock that will eventually make possible the return of Przewalski's horses to the wild.

GREAT INDIAN RHINOCEROS
Rhinoceros unicornis

A relic of prehistoric days, the great Indian rhinoceros almost seems a creature from another world. Its thick hide hangs over a bulky frame in folds that suggest armor plate. Rough warts, or protuberances, on the skin remind one of rivets. With a shoulder height sometimes well over five feet, and a weight of two tons, the overall impression is of a living tank. Indeed, Indian rulers in ancient days are said to have used the rhinoceros in warfare, fastening an iron trident over the animal's horn. If kept under control, the terrifying beast undoubtedly could move everything in its path.

The horn of the rhinoceros has long been prized as an aphrodisiac, and this belief has contributed significantly to the animal's endangered status. The horn has no bony core. It is composed of compressed fibrous material attached at the base to a rough supporting area of skin. Growing continuously, horns have measured up to two feet in length and may weigh as much as three pounds. Considered as precious as gold, rhino horn sometimes sells for more than $500 a pound. Little wonder that even though the animal is legally protected, it is often killed just for the horn, which is then sold on the black market at fabulous prices.

In times past the species had other supposed attributes that made it a handsome prize for poachers. Rhinoceros blood was believed to speed departing souls on their way to life after death, the urine was said to be an excellent disinfectant, and drinking vessels made from the horn allegedly rendered poisons harmless.

In the years 1971 and 1972, poachers killed twenty-nine of an estimated sixty Indian rhinos in the Jaldapara Reserve in West Bengal. Several years before, seven rhino poachers, caught in the act, were reportedly slain in a pitched battle at this Indian sanctuary.

The range of the great Indian rhinoceros once covered much of northern India and Nepal. Today, however, the species has disappeared from great portions of these areas, which have been cleared for timber and agricultural uses, and is now usually found only in protected sanctuaries. As many as a thousand may survive.

India has set aside eight sanctuaries for the species, the principal one being Kaziranga Sanctuary, about 166 square miles of refuge located on the south bank of the Brahmaputra River in Assam. A valley that is periodically flooded, Kaziranga is a swampy area full of tall elephant grass and rushes.

Besides the eight preserves in India, there is one in Nepal—the Chitawan Sanctuary—which protects an estimated seventy rhinos.

In 1974, there were fifty-seven great Indian rhinoceroses in twenty-nine zoological collections around the world. Twenty-seven of them were born in captivity, one of them that year.

SNOW LEOPARD
Panthera uncia

Considered by many as the most beautiful of all the cats, the snow leopard has a luxurious coat of pale smoky gray that shades to white on the undersides, with numerous black splashes and rosettes on the body. The tail is long and thick and fluffy, and the eyes, as described by zoologist George Schaller: "Pale, with a frosty glitter softened only by a twinge of amber . . . the eyes of a creature used to immense solitudes and snowy wastes."

The habitat of the snow leopard includes the high steppes and slopes of the mountains of central Asia, from Afghanistan, Pakistan, and Kashmir, to Mongolia, Tibet, and western China. A solitary and nocturnal animal, it preys on musk deer, wild sheep and goats, hares, and other small game. Driven by hunger during the harsh winters, it sometimes leaves the high slopes and descends into the valleys, where it may feed on domestic stock.

Nominally protected in much of its range, it is hunted as a destructive predator in some areas. Possessing one of the most beautiful coats in the world, the species is still taken for its fur, in spite of the fact that the International Fur Trade Federation agreed in 1971 to a voluntary ban among its members on the use of snow leopard pelts.

Today there may be one hundred snow leopards left in Pakistan. No one knows how many survive in China, Mongolia, and central Asia. Its numbers are declining everywhere, and it is presently classified as a species in imminent danger of extinction.

The zoos of the world have one hundred or more captive snow leopards, probably a significant percentage of the total population in the wild. Today these zoos are much more successful in breeding this beautiful species than they were in the past. In 1971, for example, thirty-one cubs were born to captive specimens.

ASIATIC LION
Panthera leo persica

The lion has long been considered the king of beasts, a living symbol of power and majesty. A large male lion, with his imposing mane and tawny coat, certainly commands respect, and even fear, especially if the beast is angry. Then his eyes seem to glow with fierce light, his tail twitches menacingly, and his lips draw back in a snarl. He may roar, showing his enormous teeth. Noisiest of all cats, the lion vents its feelings with what the explorer Samuel Baker has described as "awe-inspiring notes, like the rumble of distant thunder."

In ancient times the lion ranged widely over much of the Old

World, including some parts of eastern Europe. When Xerxes, the Persian conqueror, marched through Macedonia in 480 B.C., some of his baggage camels were killed by lions, as recorded by Herodotus, the Greek historian. Many lions, he noted, could be found in Thrace at that time. By A.D. 100 the big cats had disappeared from Europe, killed off by man.

Lions, however, were a familiar sight to the Romans. They imported them from North Africa and the Mideast by the hundreds, and they featured them in their numerous circus spectaculars. By the time of Augustus, as recorded by the Greek geographer Strabo, there were so few lions in Libya as a result of the Roman captures, that the inhabitants of that North African country could engage in agriculture with comparatively little fear of attack from the big cats.

The lion was still common in the Near East during Biblical times, but it disappeared from Palestine by the thirteenth century, at about the same time that Marco Polo was heading for China. In Iraq, the last lion was seen in the early 1800s, and in Pakistan the last reported killing of a lion was in 1842. A few persisted in Persia until this century, with several sightings recorded as late as 1942.

Once widely spread throughout India, the Asiatic lion, like the tiger, furnished royal sport to Indian princes and colonial nabobs alike. Colonel George Acland Smith boasted that he had shot 300 Indian lions during the mid-1800s. With such attrition, the lion had disappeared from the entire Indian Peninsula by the 1880s except for a few survivors in the Gir Forest, in the State of Gujarat in southwest India. There they seemed to be making their last stand, and in the 1890s the British naturalist Richard Lydekker stated: "A few years will probably witness the extinction of the lion throughout the peninsula."

The Nawab of Junagarh held jurisdiction over the Gir Forest, and in 1900 he extended complete protection to the lions there. The estimated population of the big cats at that time was fewer than one hundred—some said perhaps only twenty-five animals.

Under protection, the population slowly increased to about three hundred by 1950. In 1957, three of these lions were captured and taken to the Chandraprabha Sanctuary in the northern state of Uttar Pradesh, where they were released with the hope that they would start a new colony. Since that time these transplanted lions have increased quite satisfactorily.

In the Gir Forest, however, the lion population has been reduced because of habitat destruction. A century ago the Gir Forest covered three quarters of a million acres. Today it has shrunk to the 300,000 acres that compose the Gir Wildlife Sanctuary. Once the forest had many teak and other hardwood trees, but most have long since been cut down for lumber. And from time to time groups of seminomadic people invade the sanctuary with their domestic flocks of thousands of grazing animals. Serious habitat destruction has resulted, and today much of the forest has deteriorated to scrub, with encroaching areas of semidesert around its borders. Such land supports very little food or cover for the lions. And as overgrazing by domestic animals has caused the disappearance of the lions' natural wild prey—water buffalo and deer—the big cats have turned to attacking domestic stock. In retaliation, the pastoral tribes wage war against the lions.

One result of this deteriorating spiral is that the 1970 lion population of the Gir Forest had dwindled to about 170 animals. In 1972, concerned officials of the state of Gujarat launched an active conservation program designed to save the lion. The World Wildlife Fund assisted in this effort, and wildlife experts from the IUCN, The Smithsonian Institution, and Yale University cooperated in conducting studies of the habits and requirements of the Asiatic lion. Today the pastoral people and their flocks are barred from the Gir Sanctuary, and in time the forest habitat may recover. Meanwhile, the lions are being vigilantly protected in this, their last Asian stronghold.

The Asiatic lion is the only race that is seriously threatened at the moment. But two African races—the Barbary lion of North Africa and the Cape lion of South Africa—have both been exterminated at the hand of man. Populations of the big cat are dwindling in many other parts of Africa as well. The lion will eventually disappear everywhere unless man reassesses his attitude toward this magnificent creature.

TIGER
Panthera tigris

In his *Book,* Marco Polo reported that there were beautiful "striped lions" in the Szechwan and Yunnan areas of China, and that the great Kublai Khan sometimes used them in the hunt. Marco Polo had evidently never seen a tiger before, but the Romans of some fifteen hundred years earlier were well acquainted with the beasts. They imported tigers for their spectacles and pitted them against other beasts or gladiators. With the fall of the Roman Empire, however, tigers disappeared for many centuries from western Europe.

Originally the tiger ranged from the Caucasus across all of Asia, north as far as Siberia, Mongolia, and Korea, and south through the jungles of China, India, and Malaya, and the islands of Sumatra, Java, and Bali. Today the Balinese tiger is probably extinct, and the Javanese tiger very nearly so.

Throughout its traditional range the tiger is divided into eight races or subspecies. Today the IUCN lists six of them as endangered, and the other two as vulnerable. Siberian and Manchurian tigers are the largest, some weighing as much as 650 pounds. They are pale and have long fur coats to protect them against the harsh northern winters. Bengal tigers, the best-known form, are almost as large and have a more richly colored coat.

The island forms tend to be somewhat smaller and darker. Albino tigers and melanistic individuals have also been recorded.

Unlike the lion, the tiger is usually a solitary cat, although females and their young may travel together for several years. They hunt mostly at night, and their victims range from small animals to deer and wild pigs, which are their favorite prey. Domestic stock and water buffalo are also frequently taken. After making a kill, the tiger may cover and hide the carcass after eating its fill, and then return for several days until the meat is finished. Such predictable behavior has gained a tiger trophy for many a hunter.

Today wild tigers are in a crisis status throughout their range. India, the home of the Bengal tiger, now probably has fewer than two thousand of the beasts within its borders, whereas it boasted forty thousand or more a half century ago. The unique races of tiger once found in Bali, Java, and the Caucasus are either extinct today or exist only in very small numbers. The

population of the Sumatran tiger shrinks alarmingly every year. Tigers have almost completely disappeared from Korea, and in China and Siberia they are very rare. The Indochinese race of tiger still numbers perhaps two or three thousand, in spite of war and hunting and jungle defoliation. But its population is fast being reduced too. If the present trend continues, the species may well have disappeared completely in the wild by the year 2000.

Why have tiger populations diminished so drastically in recent years? The answer would have to include hunting, poisoning, the fur trade, elimination of natural prey, and—above all—destruction of habitat.

In the former days of colonial India, tiger hunting was the sport supreme for British colonials and big-game hunters from all over the world, as well as the royal pastime of native princes and maharajahs. George Schaller, who has studied the tiger in its natural habitat, mentions a maharajah who wrote to him in 1965, saying, "My total bag of tigers is only 1150." Only? The statement sounds almost apologetic, as though the maharajah is ashamed that he has not bagged more tigers as perhaps some of his fellow princes had done. But that kill, as recorded by a single hunter, probably represents at least half the total number of tigers living in India today.

In areas where they live close to man, tigers still prey on livestock such as cattle, buffalo, or goats. Sometimes they attack man himself, and the danger from the big cats is still real in certain areas. Between 1967 and 1971, for example, an average of seventy-six people a year were killed by tigers in the Sunderbans district at the mouth of the Ganges River. Schaller concludes: "Man and tiger cannot coexist. Tigers kill livestock and occasionally man himself . . . . man-eating is very rare, (but) as deep-seated fear of the cat nevertheless exists, the potential danger is real, and the killing of a tiger still confers status on the hunter, no matter how unsportingly it is done."

Illegal hunting and poaching have always been a factor in the killing of tigers. Although the taking of tigers for the fur trade has now been outlawed over most of its range, the hides and other parts of the animal are still highly valued, and prices of up to $10,000 have reportedly been paid in recent years for a single skin.

As the human population increases in India, Southeast Asia, and other tiger territory, the areas of suitable habitat for the big cats shrink year by year. As this process continues, tigers are steadily pushed into tiny pockets of their former range.

Actions are being taken, however, to reverse this trend and to protect and preserve those tigers that remain. In 1970, India imposed a five-year ban on tiger hunting. Two years later it made the tiger its national animal instead of the lion. That same year the newly established nation of Bangladesh claimed the tiger as its national emblem, too, and banned all killing.

In 1973, India launched an even more ambitious six-year program, Project Tiger, and pledged some thirty-five million rupees to a national campaign to conserve the tiger by establishing up to fifty special sanctuaries in forests and national parks. Each sanctuary, from 100 to 5000 square miles in area, may become the home of some fifty tigers. Some tigers live in the designated areas already. Others will be trapped and transported there from isolated forest habitats.

To date, India has set aside nine specific sanctuaries. The first, Corbett National Park, was proclaimed as a tiger sanctuary in April, 1973. That same year the World Wildlife Fund launched Operation Tiger, a wildlife conservation program set up to aid this species and designed to raise at least $1,000,000 for tiger conservation. Most of the funds that are being raised will be used to establish large reserves where tigers can live under protection and not in conflict with man.

Besides these conservation programs, one other factor deserves mention: the number of tigers in captivity. This captive reservoir may prove very important for the future. In 1974, according to the *International Zoo Yearbook,* there were a grand total of 539 Bengal tigers in the world's zoos (381 zoo-bred); 404 Siberian tigers (359 of these bred in captivity); 125 Sumatran tigers (of which 102 were zoo-bred); 27 Indochinese tigers (17 zoo-bred); 5 Chinese tigers (3 zoo-born); and one zoo-born Javan tiger. Probably there were also many tigers in Chinese and other Asiatic zoos, as well as many in circuses and private collections that were not counted in this tabulation.

Such captive specimens help insure the future of the species. But tigers—or any species—in captivity can never take the place of those living wild and free in their homeland. It is hoped that enough large preserves can be established in the next few years to safeguard populations of wild tigers in all of the countries and regions where they are still found. Each individual tiger, it is believed, needs about ten square miles of suitable habitat in order to sustain itself and breed.

PHEASANTS
Family Phasianidae

In 1881, the American Consul General in Shanghai, China, Judge O. N. Denny, sent thirty ring-necked pheasants to Oregon to be set free in the Willamette Valley. In later years further releases were made in New Jersey, Massachusetts, and other eastern states. Most of these introduced birds thrived, and today many millions of ring-necked pheasants roam the northern United States, coast to coast. This introduced Asiatic species is a favorite of hunters, who shoot them by the hundreds of thousands every year. The ring-neck has flourished in America.

The same cannot be said for many species of pheasant in their natural Old World habitat. All in all, the pheasant family includes forty-nine species, every one of which, except the Congo

peacock of Africa, are native to mainland Asia or to islands off
its coasts. Pheasants have always been highly prized, not only
for their flesh but also for their beautiful iridescent plumage. As
a result, their numbers have been hard pressed, for Asian nations do not raise the birds on game farms for later release in
the wild, as we often do in the United States. During the past
quarter of a century, too, much of the pheasants' Asian habitat
has been destroyed by lumbering and agricultural activities. At
the present time at least sixteen species are listed as very rare or
endangered.

Mikado pheasant

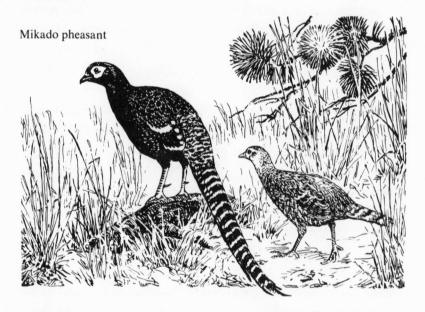

Mikado and Swinhoe's pheasants of Taiwan are now reduced
to remnant populations. One biologist who has conducted research on these species during the past several years reports:
"Some villages earned as much as $20,000 a year trapping
pheasants for sale to Chinese animal dealers. For other villagers,
the pheasants provided feathers for use in headdresses or meat
for the table." A number of other endangered species found on

the mainland are fast disappearing for much the same reasons.

Pheasants have long been favorite birds of aviculturalists, however, and captive breeding may offer the best chance at the present time to safeguard these endangered species until they can be released under more favorable conditions in their native habitats. The example of the ring-neck pheasant in America shows the feasibility of such a program.

All except one species of pheasant has been kept successfully in captivity, and all except five species have been bred successfully under these conditions. ". . . so well do pheasants respond to skilled modern management in captivity," one pheasant enthusiast has declared, that there is ". . . every prospect that the remaining species may soon successfully rear young and multiply in aviculture."

In 1959, Philip Wayre, an English aviculturalist, created the Ornamental Pheasant Trust for just this purpose. He located the Trust on his own farm close to the little town of Great Witchingham, near Norfolk, England, and donated his own pheasants of eleven different species as a breeding nucleus. In 1975, the Pheasant Trust commemorated its first fifteen years by bringing the total of rare pheasants bred at the farm to more than one thousand birds. The Trust has more than thirty species of pheasants today, including Edward's pheasant. This bird is known only from Vietnam and may now be extinct in the wild. Altogether six endangered pheasant species are breeding regularly at the Trust.

One of the Trust's goals is to send some of the surplus stock back to Asia for release in their native habitat. "This depends," as one pheasant breeder observes, "on persuading Asian conservationists and governments to provide suitable reserves for the birds." In 1967, fifteen pairs of Swinhoe's were returned to Taiwan, followed by another six pairs in 1968. Plans are presently being made to return Mikado pheasants to Taiwan as well. Cheer pheasants were sent to India in 1971 and 1972 for release in forest preserves near Simla, and six pairs each of white-crested, Kalij, and Himalayan monal pheasants have been sent to Pakistan.

Other Asian Animals Today

Today Asia is a vast continent in ferment as its human populations strive to build better lives for themselves under difficult circumstances. The booming birth rate—in India especially, but in most other Asian nations as well—adds many more millions of hungry mouths each year to those that already must be fed. By the year 2000 an estimated 3.8 billion people—very close to the population of the entire world today—will struggle for existence in Asia.

Since World War II there has been a large-scale introduction of Western technology and agricultural practices into the continent, to help the Asian nations cope with the problems of too many people, too little food, and antiquated methods of agriculture, sanitation, and health care. Vast areas of the continent—particularly Indochina and Southeast Asia—have been wracked by long wars that have destroyed a great deal of forest and cropland. Many clearing and drainage projects have been instituted, and huge areas have been sprayed with DDT and other pesticides for disease and pest control. As one inevitable result of all these activities, there has been a grave reduction of natural habitat throughout the continent. The effects of this loss on native wildlife have been dramatic.

The large-hoofed mammals show the trends most graphically. Mainland Asia is the homeland of at least five different species of wild cattle, all of which are now in serious danger. The water buffalo has been domesticated for thousands of years, but today's wild herds are mere remnant populations threatened with imminent extermination. The yak, another species long domesticated by tribes of the central highlands and used for meat, milk, and as a beast of burden, has also been almost exterminated in the wild. The gaur, or seladang, of Southeast Asia, biggest of all the world's cattle, survives only in scattered bands, as does the banteng of Burma and Indonesia. The kouprey, discovered by science as recently as 1937 by a French hunter and veterinarian, Dr. R. Sauvel, may already be extinct. Native only to Cambodia and neighboring areas, it dwindled from an estimated population of one thousand in 1940 to no more than thirty to seventy several years ago. Armies and warfare have meanwhile swept through its jungle habitat.

Many Asiatic deer besides those already mentioned are in danger of extinction. The beautiful barasingha, or swamp deer, of India has declined drastically in recent years due to hunting and loss of habitat to crops and domestic stock. So has the browantlered, or Eld's deer. This species is notable for its unusual antlers, in which the long brow tine and the beam form an unbroken sweeping curve, somewhat like the rocker on a rocking chair. The Manipur race of this unique deer today numbers no more than fifty individuals. The Thailand race, which ranges from Thailand into Indochina, has had its numbers dangerously reduced by overhunting, clearing of the forests, and the use of defoliants and other environmentally damaging operations during the long Vietnam War.

At least four Asiatic races of the red deer, a close relative of our American elk, or wapiti, are either extinct today or imminently threatened with that fate, principally because of overhunting.

A number of races of the beautiful little spotted sika deer of East Asia's mainland and islands are also in danger of extermination. The Formosan sika, for example, is restricted to the central mountains of Taiwan, where it is still hunted for food, although afforded nominal protection. Probably no more than three hundred survive in the wild, but nearly four hundred exist in captive herds today in some thirty zoos around the world.

Although the saiga now prospers under effective management, the same cannot be said for various other Asiatic antelope. The fleet and once-abundant blackbuck of India has practically disappeared due to excessive hunting, poaching, and loss of suitable habitat. So have the Arabian and Dorcus gazelles, dainty little antelopes of the Arabian Peninsula and neighboring areas.

Asia is the ancestral homeland of many magnificent wild sheep and goats, and it still supports populations of various races of the ibex, the markhor, the bharal, the Argali, and the takin (one of the goat antelopes) in remote and mountainous areas. All of these animals have long been pursued for their meat or as hunting trophies, and their populations are either decreasing or barely holding their own.

The same can be said for the various races of the Asiatic wild ass, several of which may soon disappear. The Syrian wild ass has been almost exterminated by Bedouin tribesmen, and the Indian wild ass now numbers fewer than four hundred animals, restricted to the Gujurat-Pakistan border region.

A half century ago the Malay tapir was widespread and fairly common from Burma to Malaya and Sumatra. Today this black-and-white animal is seldom seen anywhere. In Sumatra, where special preserves have been created to protect it, no more than forty to fifty individuals remain.

Besides the snub-nosed monkey, other endangered primates include the attractive lion-tailed macaque, or wanderoo monkey, which is found only in a localized area of the western Ghats in India. Fewer than one thousand of them are believed to survive. Two other vanishing species are the golden langur of the Assam-Bhutan border, and the Douc langur of Indochina and Hainan.

Smallest and perhaps the most appealing of the great apes, the gibbons of southeast Asia and some of the islands of Malaysia have been perilously reduced by illegal hunting, capture for the zoo and pet trade, and for research. Gibbons live in small family groups in well-defined territories, and many adults are killed by hunters in order to capture young ones.

Many of Asia's birds, particularly the large and spectacular species that are prized for their flesh or plumage, are declining rapidly. The Asiatic white stork—either a race of the European white stork, or a closely related but distinct species—is probably doomed. This bird now numbers no more than several hundred individuals in the vast eastern continent. They are found in scattered localities in China, Siberia, and North Korea. As late as 1962 there were twenty Asiatic white storks in Japan, but they were unsuccessful in nesting and their numbers dwindled. Many people blame the failure to breed on the buildup of DDT and other pesticides in the bodies of the amphibians and other small animals that are the stork's prey. Whatever the cause, the white stork has now disappeared entirely in Japan.

One of Asia's most densely populated and highly industrialized nations, Japan, has long used many insecticides that are undoubtedly affecting the reproductive cycles of birds such as the stork and the Japanese crested ibis, which numbered only about twenty-five individuals in 1965. The magnificent Japanese crane is very rare and declines in population year by year. Ten years ago there were fewer than two hundred of them in Japan, plus a few more in Russian Siberia. Hunting, drainage, and disturbance by man seem to be the destructive factors, as with the whooping crane in America. The Siberian white crane is also decreasing rapidly for the same reasons. The Chinese egret is very rare and may be extinct. It was almost exterminated by plume hunters in the past, but now it seems to be succumbing to pollutants and loss of habitat.

Asia's crocodilians—the marsh crocodile of Southeast Asia, the Siamese crocodile, the Indian gavial, and the Chinese alligator—are all presently endangered by heavy hunting and poaching for their hides. Many snakes, the spectacular big pythons in particular, are also being killed for their beautiful skins.

The endangered species listed here are but a few of those that may disappear within the next few years. As a result of human pollution, destruction of natural habitat, widespread hunting and poaching, and the drenching of vast areas with insecticides, increasing numbers of wildlife species will be exterminated unless more sanctuaries and protective measures are instituted.

Where the south declines toward the setting sun lies Ethiopia. There gold is obtained in great plenty, huge elephants abound . . . and the men are taller and longer-lived than anywhere else. Herodotus

4

AFRICA, LAND OF THE LAST GREAT HERDS

The ancient Mediterranean civilizations knew Africa only as a vast, undefined land of mystery to the south. Phoenicians and other seafarers skirted its coasts; sometimes they landed and traded with native tribes. The ancient Egyptians knew the fertile borders of their mighty Nile River as far as the third or fourth cataract, several hundred miles inland, but little more. The sources of that mighty river were not learned until the nineteenth century. These early civilizations were curious to discover Africa's secrets, and bit by bit they began to uncover them.

The Phoenicians, chief sailors of the ancients, founded Carthage on Africa's north rim about 900 B.C. and sailed their ships both east and west on voyages of exploration. The ancient

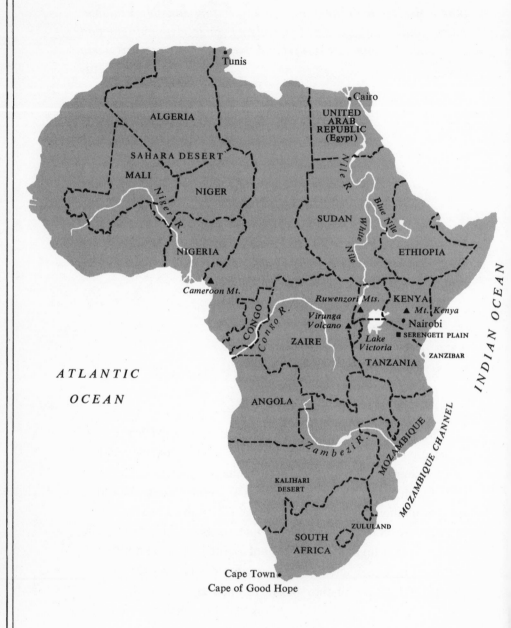

Tunis

ALGERIA

Cairo

UNITED
ARAB
REPUBLIC
(Egypt)

SAHARA DESERT

MALI

NIGER

Niger R.

Nile R.

Blue Nile

SUDAN

White Nile

ETHIOPIA

NIGERIA

Cameroon Mt.

Ruwenzori Mts.

KENYA

Mt. Kenya

Congo R.

CONGO

Virunga
Volcano

Nairobi

*Lake
Victoria*

SERENGETI PLAIN

ZAIRE

TANZANIA

ZANZIBAR

ATLANTIC

OCEAN

ANGOLA

Zambezi R.

MOZAMBIQUE

MOZAMBIQUE CHANNEL

INDIAN OCEAN

KALIHARI
DESERT

ZULULAND

SOUTH
AFRICA

Cape Town

Cape of Good Hope

AFRICA

Egyptians also sought to learn more about the lands outside their sphere. About the year 600 B.C., Necho, King of Egypt, repaired an already ancient canal that linked the Nile to the Red Sea and sent forth an expedition manned by Phoenicians to explore the African coastline. Heading southward on the prevailing winds, the expedition lasted for two years, as recorded by Herodotus. Sailing clockwise around Africa, the expedition finally returned to Egypt through the Straits of Gibraltar and the Mediterranean Sea. Even though he recorded this remarkable voyage, Herodotus found it hard to believe. A similar voyage around Africa in the opposite direction did not take place until more than twenty centuries later.

Exploring Unknown Coasts

About 500 B.C., the Phoenician Hanno sailed from Carthage through the Straits of Gibraltar and southward along the west coast of Africa. Passing the delta of the River Niger, he ventured as far as Cameroon Mountain, just above the equator in present-day Cameroon. Hanno recorded seeing live volcanoes and visiting an island with strange, hairy savages on it, which the interpreter for the expedition called "gorillae." Three of these animals were killed, and their skins brought back to Carthage, where— as reported by Herodotus—they were preserved in the temple of Astarte until the Romans conquered the Carthaginians several hundred years later. Whether they were actually gorilla skins or those of some lesser ape, no one will ever know.

The Romans finally defeated their Carthaginian rivals in 146 B.C., at the end of the Third Punic War. After conquering Egypt as well, they ruled the Mediterranean world for several hundreds of years thereafter. Hanno's voyage to Cameroon, however, was not duplicated, as far as we know, until the fifteenth century when the Portuguese began to probe farther and farther southward along Africa's West Coast.

In 1487, Bartolomeo Diaz sailed as far as the Cape of Good Hope, near Africa's southern tip, before turning back. Ten years later Vasco da Gama sailed past the Cape and on to Zanzibar, proving once and for all that Africa was a great continent with open ocean to the south of it.

The island of Zanzibar had long been a flourishing trading center. Strategically located on the shores of the Indian Ocean below the horn of eastern Africa, it served as an outlet for slaves, ivory, and other goods from Africa's interior, as well as a depot for products from both the Mediterranean and the Far East. Arab navigators were probably the first to sail the monsoons across the Indian Ocean to India and the Orient, but in time the Phoenicians, Greeks, and Romans learned the secret, too.

Below Africa's narrow green strip of Mediterranean coast-land lies the vast Sahara Desert, which acted as a highly effective barrier to inland exploration by the Phoenicians, Greeks, and Romans. Toward the end of the Ice Age, however, the area had been pleasant and productive grassland, the home of many tribes and wild animals. But, four to six thousand years ago, the grass-lands began to dry up, possibly because of the changing climate or owing to man's habit of overtilling and overgrazing the land. Gradually the desert spread, replacing the fertile land. Here and there were palm-shaded oases, separated by hundreds of miles of barren dunes. Hardy desert tribes and their dromedaries traveled the caravan routes that connected the oases, but few others ventured into the wastes of burning sands. Timbuctoo, the fabled city at the crossroads of these caravan trails, was only a vague reference to fifteenth-century Europeans.

The Source of the Nile

The valley of the Nile, however, was another matter. As early as 700 B.C., the Egyptians had explored the Nile valley as far as the fourth cataract, where the Blue Nile comes out of the mountains of Ethiopia and joins the White Nile. Today the Sudanese city of Khartoum lies in the fork. They had also explored parts of Ethiopia. Herodotus, who visited much of the known world of his day, ascended the Nile as far as Aswan—the first cataract—in 470 B.C. and speculated about the river's source. Several hundred years later Ptolemy of Egypt claimed that the sources of the river were twin lakes fed by legendary Mountains of the Moon.

Emperor Nero attempted to solve the riddle about A.D. 60, when he sent Roman centurions on a voyage of exploration. The Roman writer Seneca, in his *Quaestiones Naturales,* reported that ". . . I have had an opportunity of hearing the report of the two centurions sent by the Emperor Nero to the sources of the Nile. . . . We came, they reported, to immense swamps, the area of which is unknown even to the natives and which no one can tell. For the water plants there are so closely intertwined that no one can measure this water, either on foot or in a boat. . . . There we espied two rocks, between which the Nile gushed forth in mighty fulness."

The enterprising centurions thus added some additional bits to the already existing knowledge about the Nile, but they were evidently not the first Europeans to pass this way. Nearly a century before, a Greek merchant, Diogenes, is said to have left a place called Rhapta—an East African coastal settlement, perhaps not far from Zanzibar—and ". . . travelled inland for 25-days journey and arrived in the vicinity of two great lakes, and the snowy range of mountains whence the Nile draws its twin sources."

The ancients came close indeed to learning the sources of the Nile, but not until the nineteenth century did explorers settle the matter to the satisfaction of Victorian geographers.

Modern Exploration of Africa

The industrious Portuguese were the first to build a way station and fort at the Cape of Good Hope. They were displaced in 1652, however, by the Dutch, who promptly began the settlement of South Africa. During the next two centuries almost all of the continent was brought under the colonial yoke as many European countries vied for territory and commercial benefits. In the process, the continent was opened up and its secrets explored.

Determined to solve the puzzle of the Nile's source, the English explorers Richard Burton and John Speke struck inland from Zanzibar in 1857 and the following year reached Lake Tanganyika, where Burton fell ill. Speke pushed on by himself to find Lake Victoria, which he proclaimed as the true source of the Nile. Four years later Speke made his way into Uganda, where he reached the left bank of the Nile at the mighty Ripon Falls.

Less than ten years later another Victorian explorer, Samuel Baker, discovered Lake Albert and the Murchison Falls, where "the river drops in one leap 120 feet into a deep basin, the edge of which literally swarms with crocodiles."

Meanwhile, the noted missionary-explorer David Livingstone was blazing new trails for Europeans through the southern half of the continent. Sent to Bechuanaland in 1840, ". . . determined to open up the country . . ." he crossed the Kalahari Desert and explored the Zambesi River during the next fifteen years, and in 1854 mounted an expedition into the Congo basin, eventually opening up a trade route across Africa from the Atlantic to the Indian Ocean.

During the same period, an American explorer, Henry Stanley, was surveying Lakes Victoria and Tanganyika and discovering Lake Edward. Stanley followed the Congo down its course and rediscovered Ptolemy's Mountains of the Moon. He also made much of the fact that he had "found" the missing

David Livingstone, who had not really been lost in the first place.

Finally one enterprising individual, Edward Scott Grogan, became the first human being of record to traverse Africa from the Cape to Cairo, following the whole Nile Basin. Traveling mostly on foot, the rugged Grogan completed the project in one and a half years.

The Land and People

Today the land and people of Africa are well-known, and so are its animals, although there are those who say that some of its zoological marvels are still undiscovered. Since World War II, the many nations of the continent have to a great extent broken their colonial ties, and all of them are endeavoring to build better lives for their peoples.

The people that inhabit the continent are as varied as the regions they live in, for the story of man in Africa is a complicated but fascinating one. It began with the records left in the rocks, showing that early man lived in Africa millions of years ago. Its mysteries only recently explored by Western man, Africa was the birthplace of one of the first great civilizations—ancient Egypt. Other highly developed civilizations also arose thousands of years ago in the Arab lands of North Africa and in the legendary interior kingdom of Ethiopia.

South of the Sahara, Africa harbors a great diversity of people with widely divergent physical attributes, languages, and cultures. They are as varied as the nomadic Masai of the East African plains, who measure their wealth in cattle; the advanced, warlike Kikuyu; and the primitive Pygmies who live in the equatorial rain forests with a Stone Age culture. South Africa harbors the equally primitive Bushmen, who hunt and forage in the hostile desert areas of the Kalahari Desert. In South Africa are also the proud Zulus, who early in the nineteenth century united with other Bantu tribes under the dynamic leader Shaka, and carved

out a powerful empire before the coming of the European colo-
nizers.

Today these diverse Africans face a bewildering number of
problems—problems complicated by rising populations, the colonial past, and above all by the facts of geography. Africa's lands
are bordered by the vast Sahara Desert in the north and the
Kalahari Desert in the southwest, which merge into wooded
steppes and extensive grasslands and plains on either side of the
vast rain forests of the Congo. The southern end of the continent
is a varied country, with coastal swamps and grasslands backed
up by mountains and semidesert areas, as well as productive
croplands in the interior. All of these habitats affect both the
wild animals and the people that live in them. Today Africa still
has the greatest herds of wildlife left in the world, but they are
fast dwindling under the relentless pressures of change.

The heart of Africa's wildlife country is the rich grassland
area of East Africa—the plains and wooded savannahs of Kenya
and Tanzania. There is the great Rift Valley, where some of the
earliest human beings lived millions of years ago. There are the
great lakes of Africa: Victoria, Albert, and Edward—the sources
of the Nile—as well as Lakes Tanganyika and Nyasa. There are
snow-capped Mount Kilimanjaro and Mount Kenya; and beyond
them the Virunga Volcanoes, where Zaire, Uganda, and Rwanda
meet, and the Ruwenzori Range, the fabled Mountains of the
Moon.

There, too, are the world's last great herds of wild animals—
elephants and buffalo, gnus, wildebeest, and antelopes of many
kinds. There are the predators that follow the herds—lions,
leopards, cheetahs, hyenas, Cape hunting dogs, and great birds
of prey. There are many of the national parks and preserves—
Serengeti, Albert, Murchison Falls, Tsavo, and others. Such
parks are vitally needed, for the wildlife of Africa is making its
last stand against man's relentless challenge.

AFRICAN ELEPHANT
Loxodonta africana

A huge African elephant bulldozes its way through thick brush, heading for a water hole. Pausing, it lifts its trunk and trumpets loudly. Then it crashes onward, and the earth trembles. Like no other animal, the African elephant is a beast that inspires awe.

It is even bigger than the Asiatic elephant and has larger fan-shaped ears. Instead of a back elevated in the middle, like that of the Asiatic species, the African elephant has a shoulder and a rump elevation, with a dip between the two. A big bull may weigh six or seven tons, stand eleven feet high at the shoulder, and carry tusks as long as nine or ten feet; the record goes to a pair about eleven feet long and weighing 293 pounds.

These awesome beasts once ranged over much of Africa, from the southern rim of the Sahara to the Cape of Good Hope. In ancient times they were tamed and trained for use in battle, especially during the period of the Punic Wars between Rome and Carthage. In 251 B.C., the Romans captured 100 African elephants from the Carthaginians at Palermo. The victorious Roman general, Lucius Metellus, had them ferried across the Sicilian Straits on rafts built with floating barrels. They were then exhibited in many Roman towns in celebration of the victory. The great Carthaginian leader Hannibal retaliated for this insult when he led his armies and elephants across the Alps in 218 B.C. and defeated the Romans at the battle of Cannae. And a year later African elephants played an important role in a battle waged in the Sinai Desert between Seleucus Antiochus III of Syria and Ptolemy IV of Egypt. The Egyptians finally won the day, even though their African elephants were reportedly terrified by the better-trained Indian elephants.

Such ancient wartime use of African elephants declined, and the art of capturing and training the beasts was evidently discontinued many centuries ago. It was reinstituted in 1900, however, when an enterprising Belgian colonial official named Jules LaPlume established an Elephant Domestication Station at Vira-Vungo in the northeastern Belgian Congo (now Zaire). Initially a pet project of King Leopold of Belgium, the station flourished for many years and is still in operation. William Bridges of the New York Zoological Society visited it in 1947 and reported that thirty to forty elephants were received there for training every year, most of them captured in nearby Garamba National Park by special permission. The hunters carefully singled out young and vulnerable elephants for capture. The youngster was seized in any way possible and quickly hobbled with loops of rope around its feet until it was helpless. A tame monitor elephant was then brought up and teamed with the smaller wild one. Subdued, the captive was taken back to camp where the long process of taming and training it began. When an elephant graduated from the course, it was put to work on a plantation.

In 1947, there were as many as 200,000 elephants in the Belgian Congo. But some modern elephant experts believe that Africa once supported as many as fifteen million elephants. Others put the top figure at three million. Whatever their numbers, elephants were abundant and dominant animals over much of Africa in the late nineteenth century.

Killing the beasts for their tusks was a common activity all over the continent. At least two million elephants, according to one estimate, were shot from 1880 to 1910. As early as 1861, Paul Du Chaillu observed: "Ivory comes down the river from the interior by inland journey in great quantities. Upward of 80,000 pounds are taken from the Gaboon River yearly . . . elephants must finally disappear."

Describing the scene in 1934, another hunter related that in the Sudan: "I heard of a Greek who must have been responsible for shooting over four thousand elephants in his lifetime. He had a contract to produce three hundred and fifty elephants a year as food for the mines in the Belgian Congo, for twelve years. My informant told me that he could remember the days when elephants used to pass the borders of the Belgian Congo, the Sudan, and Uganda, in herds of thousands. . . . There is no doubt that the last thirty years have seen the elephant of Africa vastly reduced by the frantic hunt for food and ivory."

Wasteful and cruel, elephant poaching has continued unabated until the present day, and perhaps it will not stop until all the elephants are gone. An estimated 10,000 elephants were killed in 1966 in the Congo alone, and in 1973 the price for ivory soared from $14 to $32 a pound. At that rate the tusks of one prime elephant alone were worth several thousand dollars. In 1974, there were perhaps 150,000 elephants in Kenya— probably about half the total in all of Africa. Every year the number grows smaller, not only because of ivory poaching but also because elephants require space that man needs for settlement and grazing his animals.

When there are too many elephants in a restricted area, they cause marked changes in the environment. "Elephants, with their path-making and tree-splitting propensities, will alter the character of the very densest brush in very short order," the American writer and naturalist Peter Matthiessen has noted. "Probably they rank with man and fire as the greatest force for habitat change in Africa. In the Serengeti, the herds are destroying many of the taller trees. . . ."

A predictable pattern unfolds when too many elephants move into an unspoiled area. Over a period of time they trample the brush and destroy most of the acacias and other trees by stripping them of bark during feeding. They move on, and native herdsmen and their cattle come in. The cattle destroy the grass by overgrazing, and the herders and cattle move on in turn. Finally the brush grows back and the cycle repeats itself, if enough time is allowed for the recovery process. But that is usually not the case in Africa today. More and more living space and agricultural lands are needed to meet the demands of a burgeoning population.

As a result of this land-and-people squeeze, African elephants are being forced out of much of their natural territory and are concentrated instead in national parks and preserves, which cannot support the huge numbers of elephants. There were 135 elephants in Kruger National Park in 1935, for example. By 1968 the population had increased to 7701 animals, many more than the area can reasonably bear. In Kenya's Tsavo National Park—one of the best elephant territories in Africa—there were about 23,000 elephants concentrated in the park in 1970, with perhaps 12,000 additional elephants in bordering areas. During the drought in 1971, 3000 elephants died of starvation and disease.

Alarmed by the trend toward greater concentrations of elephants in small areas, and by their overall dwindling populations, the International Union for the Conservation of Nature and Natural Resources (IUCN), in 1974, proposed a policy that included strict regulation of elephant hunting and ivory sale, a crackdown on poachers, and an education program to publicize the benefits of preserving some elephants. Although a certain amount of population control is necessary, experts admit, elephants remain one of Africa's greatest tourist attractions. In addition, they offer opportunities for game ranching and, therefore, should be managed and protected in numerous parks and preserves.

BLACK RHINOCEROS
Diceros bicornis

Jan van Riebeeck, the founder of the Dutch settlement at the Cape of Good Hope, noted that rhinoceroses were common there about 1650. The traveling coach of one of his successors, Simon van der Stel, was upset by a charging rhino in 1685, an act that may have contributed to its reputation for unpredictable and dangerous behavior.

The rhinoceros, like the elephant, looks prehistoric, a relic of ages past. And indeed it is. Elephants and rhinoceroses were dominant and widespread animals in the Ice Age, and those that survive today are the last representatives of ancient lines. And unless we guard them well, these survivors will have disappeared by the year 2000, known to future generations of man only through museum specimens.

Standing five to five and a half feet tall at the shoulder, the black rhino is not quite as big as its cousin, the white rhinoceros, but it is a formidable beast, weighing up to four thousand pounds. Its skin is relatively smooth and hairless, without any sign of the folds of the Indian rhinoceros. It has two horns, of which the forward is the longer. The record is slightly more than fifty-three inches. Its sight is very poor, but it has keen hearing and sense of smell to compensate. Perched on the rhino's back, oxpeckers, or tick birds, eat ticks that infest the rhino's skin and also help warn their host of danger.

Many cases in which rhinos charge human beings are the result of the beast coming closer to investigate a possible threat. On occasion, the black rhinoceros even charges automobiles and trains.

A browser, with a pointed prehensile upper lip designed for eating leaves and twigs, the black rhinoceros once ranged the open plains of Africa in great numbers, from the Cape to the southern fringe of the Sahara Desert. But during the nineteenth century, rhinos were slaughtered by the thousands for their meat and hides, as game trophies, and especially for their horns, which Asians have prized for centuries as a cure-all for many human ailments.

All five species of rhinoceros have suffered because of this belief, and as the numbers of Asian rhinos have dwindled in recent years almost to extinction, poachers have shifted more of their activity to Africa, where they receive as much as $150 a pound for rhino horn. Under such pressure, populations of the black rhinoceros have plummeted.

Today only remnant populations survive in scattered areas of their former range and on protected reserves. A 1960 survey conducted by the Survival Service Commission of the IUCN indicated that approximately 11,000 to 13,500 black rhinos still survive in Africa, with half or more concentrated in Kenya and Tanzania. In 1972, an estimated 6000 to 9000 rhinos lived in the Tsavo region of Kenya. But year by year the number shrinks. The current population of black rhinoceroses is much greater than that of the other rhinos, but the yearly decrease in their numbers is therefore much greater. Efforts to preserve them are hindered by the belief held by some people that there are still too many black rhinoceroses.

After World War II, the Kenya Game Department hired J. A. Hunter, a noted white hunter, to kill the rhinos in the Makueni District in an attempt to make 50,000 acres suitable for agricultural settlement. In all, 1088 rhinos were killed as part of this project, which eventually failed in spite of vast financial backing. The land in question was only marginal and unsuitable for growing anything except bare subsistence crops.

Granted, the rhino is an uncomfortable animal to have close to human settlement, as is the elephant or the grizzly bear. But such beasts need living space too. Their only chance for future survival is through strict protection on game preserves and in national parks. Even in such places their numbers will probably have to be controlled so that they do not overpopulate the range and destroy their food source.

WHITE, OR SQUARE-LIPPED, RHINOCEROS
Ceratotherium simum

Somewhat larger than its black relative, the white rhinoceros stands six to six and a half feet at the shoulder, measures thirteen feet or more from snout to tail, and weighs three to four tons. A grazing animal instead of a browsing one like the black rhino,

it has a square muzzle, which it uses to crop grasses. Although a slightly lighter hue than its relative, the white rhinoceros is no more "white" than its cousin is "black." Both species enjoy wallowing in mud, and their skin takes on the shade of the dried mud in the area in which they live.

Formerly ranging widely throughout southern Africa as well as in a restricted area of central Africa, the white rhino was not recognized as a distinct species or described scientifically until much later than the black. William Burchell, a noted nineteenth-century naturalist and African explorer, bagged his first white rhinoceros in 1812, near Kuruman, south of the Kalahari Desert in South Africa. Several years later he described the animal in a scientific journal and gave it its specific name, *simum*.

Throughout the nineteenth century, the white rhinoceros suffered heavily at the hands of white hunters, poachers, and Africans. Observing the hunting scene during the closing years of the nineteenth century, one famous hunter, Frederick Selous, remarked: ". . . thousands upon thousands of these huge creatures were killed by white hunters, and natives armed with the white man's weapons, and the species had become practically extinct." Selous was referring to the South African population of the white rhinoceros, the only one that was known when he started his hunting career. Almost all of this population had disappeared by the 1890s, and experts considered the species doomed. But then another population was discovered in a small area of central Africa, including the southern Sudan and adjacent parts of the Belgian Congo and Uganda. Described as a separate race, this northern population was promptly pursued by hunters and poachers in the same way that the southern race had been.

Today the northern white rhino (*C. s. cottoni*) is listed as an endangered animal with an estimated total population of from two to three hundred animals. A dozen years ago there were five or six times that many in just one preserve—the Garamba National Park in the Belgian Congo (now Zaire). Early in 1963, however, rebels from the southern Sudan invaded the park and, among other atrocities, killed off most of the white rhinos. By the end of that year the rhino population in Garamba had plummeted to under one hundred animals. In 1971, eight years later, there were only about thirty survivors in the park.

Uganda had about ninety white rhinos in its Ajai Reserve in 1971. During the early 1960s twelve animals from this reserve were captured and transplanted to Murchison Falls National Park. By 1972 they had increased their population to eighteen.

Meanwhile, in the early years of the twentieth century, a handful of survivors of the southern race were discovered living in Zululand. Under rigid protection this remnant multiplied. By 1965 the rhinos numbered over 600 at Umfolozi Game Reserve in Zululand, about 75 at nearby Hluhluwe Reserve, and 130 in neighboring areas.

This increasing population became such a heavy burden for the available habitat that a number of rhinos were captured and transported to other areas in the early 1960s. This transfer was done fairly efficiently and painlessly by shooting each rhino with a rifle-propelled dart that contained artificial morphine, which temporarily drugged the animal so that it could be checked, loaded on a truck, and moved. In this way 300 white rhinos were transplanted to various other South African parks as well as to refuges in Kenya, Rhodesia, and other African nations by 1969. Some 60 white rhinoceroses have also been sent to selected zoos. In 1974, there were 158 males and 201 females in eighty-seven different zoological collections, worldwide. Some of these animals have started to breed successfully; 9 young rhinos were born to captive specimens in 1973.

GORILLA
Gorilla gorilla

"Nearly six feet high (he proved two inches shorter), with immense body, huge chest, and great muscular arms, with fiercely glaring large deep gray eyes, and a hellish expression of face, which seemed like some nightmare vision: thus stood before us this king of the African forests.

"He was not afraid of us. He stood there, and beat his breast with his huge fists till it resounded like an immense bass drum, which is their mode of offering defiance; meantime giving vent to roar after roar . . . we fired and killed him."

Thus did explorer Paul Du Chaillu describe one of his encounters with a gorilla in the Congo forest more than a century ago, when the gorilla was a virtually unknown beast. Du Chaillu was able to observe the gorilla better than any other European of his time, but he did little to dispel the evil reputation that our nearest relative has had since primitive times.

Compare Du Chaillu's attitude with that of George Schaller, the well-known ethologist (student of animal behavior) who in 1959 and 1960 made the first detailed study of the mountain gorilla in the wild. "I was little prepared for the beauty of the beasts before me," he relates in his book *The Year of the Gorilla*.

"Their hair was not merely black, but a shining blue-black, and their black faces shone as if polished. . . . The large male . . . was the most magnificent animal I had ever seen. His brow ridges overhung his eyes, and the crest on his crown resembled a hairy miter. . . . He gave an impression of dignity and restrained power, of absolute certainty in his majestic appearance."

As demonstrated by the experiences of Schaller and other trained observers such as Dian Fossey, the gorilla is in truth a shy and reticent animal, one that lives at peace with other animals of its habitat, and with man as well, unless attacked or approached too closely. Then the gorilla may bluster and bluff, trying to scare the intruder away with short charges and breast-beatings, but only after great provocation. The two observers mentioned above lived in close contact with gorillas for months or years at a time and were never harmed. Indeed, they were finally accepted.

Dian Fossey, under a grant from the National Geographic

Society, lived near gorillas on the slopes of the Virunga Volcanoes from 1967 to 1971 and has spent thousands of hours observing them. She gained their confidence by imitating their daily activities: sampling the foods they ate, scratching herself when they scratched, and imitating their various cries. Slowly they became used to her. In 1970, she had the unique experience of having a young adult male gorilla touch her hand briefly in a curious but friendly contact before he drew back and scurried off into the forest.

"The gorilla," asserts Dian Fossey, "is one of the most maligned animals in the world." Most of this attitude has been built on ignorance, however, for until the initial studies of George Schaller, less than twenty years ago, the gorilla was one of the world's least known and most misunderstood of animals.

Gorillas usually live together in small bands of three to twenty individuals, with a mature male, or silverback, as the leader. Vegetarians, the gorillas wander from place to place feeding on leaves, fruits, and pithy stalks. At night they sleep in makeshift beds constructed of leafy boughs and other vegetation. Females and young often build their nests in the trees, but the bigger and heavier males make theirs on the ground at the base of the tree trunk. There they can act quickly as sentinels on guard.

A large male gorilla in the wild may measure five and a half feet in height and weigh 450 pounds. Adult females seldom weigh more than 250 pounds. Devoted mothers, they keep the young with them for three years or so. During a lifetime that might reach thirty years, a female may bear four or five young.

The western, or lowland, gorilla (*Gorilla g. gorilla*), the only gorilla known before this century, ranges through the tropical rain forests of West Africa from southern Nigeria to Gabon, and inland about five hundred miles almost to the Ubangi River, a tributary of the Congo. Separated from this western population by more than seven hundred miles of tropical forest, gorillas are found once again in the forests of eastern Zaire, and the Virunga Mountains at the borders of Zaire, Uganda, and Rwanda. Until about five years ago, all of these eastern gorillas were considered to belong to the race known as the mountain gorilla (*G. g. berengei*). In 1970, however, mammalogist C. P. Groves divided the eastern population into two forms, designating those living in the lowland forests of eastern Zaire as a new subspecies (*G. g. graueri*). The true mountain gorilla has an estimated population of fewer than one thousand individuals, all restricted to the slopes of the Virunga Volcanoes and nearby areas. Mountain gorillas in general can be distinguished from the lowland forms by their thicker and darker fur, narrower face, and the more pronounced crest on the head of the adult males.

Until quite recently, very little was known about how either the lowland or mountain gorilla lived. In 1896, in an attempt to gain this knowledge, one optimistic scientist named Garner built himself an iron cage in which he sat patiently day after day, in gorilla territory, waiting for the animals to come to him so that he could record their behavior. The gorillas, however, did not oblige him.

The early twentieth century was an active time for collecting gorillas for museums. From 1902 to 1925, more than fifty gorillas were taken from the Virunga Volcanoes alone. In 1921, the eminent sculptor and collector Carl Akeley shot five specimens in this area for the American Museum of Natural History in New York City. Mounted in lifelike poses in the museum's African Hall—the huge male standing and thumping his chest in full glory—the group has been observed by many millions of museum visitors.

After collecting the animals he needed for his habitat groups, Akeley persuaded the Belgian Government to set aside a gorilla sanctuary in the eastern Congo. The Albert National Park was created in 1925 and enlarged in 1929 to include the entire chain of Virunga Volcanoes that lay within the territory of the Belgian Congo.

Despite all the activity of collecting gorillas for museum exhibits and of making detailed anatomical studies, little had been discovered about the real nature of the beast—how it lived, what it ate, all the habits of its natural existence. This ignorance contributed greatly to the poor luck that plagued attempts to keep the gorilla in captivity. Only within the last thirty years or so has this species been maintained successfully and eventually bred and raised in captivity.

The honor of recording the world's first birth of a gorilla in captivity went to the Columbus Zoological Gardens in Ohio when a baby lowland gorilla was born on December 22, 1956. Within a few years many other zoos were reporting similar successes. No fewer than 17 lowland-gorilla infants were born to zoo animals in 1973, and 9 of them survived. All in all, the *1975 International Zoo Yearbook* records 54 gorillas born in captivity to date. They are included in a total of 374 lowland gorillas in 111 different collections, worldwide, and 16 mountain gorillas in 6 collections.

Everyone, all responsible zoo administrators included, would shudder to recall the former practice of killing adult gorillas to capture their young. As one zoo man wrote in 1943: ". . . the methods used heretofore in capturing young animals for exhibition have almost without exception resulted in the death of at least one adult gorilla, usually the infant's mother, and upon one excuse or another native hunters necessarily used in these expeditions have all too often managed to exterminate entire bands." George Schaller reports that sixty gorillas were killed in 1948 near Anguma, Zaire, in order to obtain eleven infants for sale. Of these young, only one survived.

Most such atrocities—insofar as they relate to capturing

gorillas for exhibition or scientific research—are happily in the past. In 1962, the American Association of Zoological Parks and Aquariums passed a resolution boycotting illegal trade in gorillas, among other endangered species. In 1969, the Endangered Species Act passed by the United States Congress banned importation of gorillas into the United States except for those brought in under special permits for scientific or educational purposes. That same year the nations of the African Convention designated the gorilla as a protected animal. And today the International Union of Directors of Zoological Gardens and other zoo federations have banned acquisition of mountain gorillas by any of their members.

At the present time the gorilla is nominally protected in a number of sanctuaries throughout its range. The first gorilla sanctuary was Albert National Park, established in 1925 and subsequently enlarged. In 1932, the nearby Kayonza Forest, which harbors a number of gorillas, was made a forest reserve; in 1961, it was upgraded to the status of a wildlife sanctuary. Since World War II, the Government of Zaire has continued, under trying circumstances, to protect the gorillas in Kayonza, as well as in Albert Park, which has been renamed Parc de Virunga.

George Schaller, Dian Fossey, and others who have studied the gorilla in its native habitat have expressed deep concern about the constant reduction in size and deterioration of the gorilla's natural habitat through human encroachment. Since the mid-1940s the areas occupied by the mountain gorilla have undergone drastic changes. Much of its habitat has been destroyed by the effects of war and an expanding human population. In 1958 some 37,000 acres were withdrawn from Zaire's Parc de Virunga for use as agricultural and grazing land. In 1968, the park was invaded by thousands of herdsmen from Rwanda with flocks of cattle. Poachers slaughtered wildlife indiscriminately, and more than a score of Congolese park staff were killed as they attempted to protect the land and wildlife.

Through the entire range of the gorilla—lowland and mountain forms alike—Africans still kill them for their meat or in retaliation for gorillas raiding gardens or plantain groves. Steadily the overall gorilla population continues to diminish.

Accurate estimates as to how many gorillas survive vary widely. Twelve years ago one scientist approximated the population at 20,000 in the Congo; at about the same time, George Schaller thought there might be as many as 5 to 15,000 in the eastern population. However, optimists today estimate a total population of 10 to 15,000 at best. The IUCN now lists the population of the mountain gorilla as fewer than 1000, and a 1972 count estimated the Virunga Volcano population at under 275.

Everywhere the steady erosion of gorilla natural living space continues as men and cattle and timbering interests destroy the forest land they need to survive. The irony will be bitter if *Homo sapiens* eliminates his nearest animal relative. But that eventuality may very well happen. "Unless a better planned and more determined effort is made to save the mountain gorilla," Dian Fossey warns, "it is doomed to extinction within the next two or three decades." Over a somewhat longer time span, the same could be said for the lowland gorilla as well.

QUAGGA
Equus quagga

Portuguese mariners were the first modern Europeans to round the Cape of Good Hope and open the ocean route to the Far East. The Dutch, however, were the ones who first settled at the Cape in 1652. It was a convenient place for ships to lay over for repairs or to stock up on food and fresh water before sailing on. Permanent settlers soon began to spread out over the land and stake out homesteads on the grasslands, or veldt, as the Boer farmers called it.

The veldt teemed with great herds of various kinds of antelope, to each of which the Dutch gave a name: springbok, blesbok, bontebok, hartebeest, and wildebeest. They also encountered great numbers of little wild horses, which the native Hottentot people called *quahkah,* accenting the last syllable in imitation of the shrill barking neighs that these animals frequently emitted. The Dutch adapted the name to quagga.

The quagga had black stripes on its head, neck, and shoulders, but the rest of its body was a light brown color with a dark brown stripe running down the middle of its back. The tail and all four legs were white. Quagga were very abundant and customarily moved about in small herds, often in association with wildebeests and ostriches. Because they competed for grass with the cattle of the settlers, the Dutch hunted them down and killed them by the thousands. The meat was used to feed slaves and farm workers, and the hides could be used for many different items.

English naturalist William Burchell witnessed a quagga hunt and roundup in 1811. Describing the sound and the fury of great herds of quagga galloping past, he wrote: "I could compare it to nothing but to the din of a tremendous charge of cavalry, or to the rushing of a mighty tempest. I could not estimate the accumulated number at less than fifteen thousand, a great extent of the country being actually chequered black and white with their congregated masses."

Not surprisingly, the quagga had disappeared from the Cape Colony by 1840, although it was still plentiful in relatively unsettled areas to the north and east. But not for long. In 1814, the Dutch had been forced to cede Cape Province to the English, and their determined desire for independence led them in 1836 to start a great trek northeastward to found the Orange Free State and the Transvaal. Once again farming and the quagga came into conflict, with the same inevitable result; by 1870 the little half zebras were gone everywhere in the wild. A few had been sent to zoos from time to time, but they were never given the right conditions for breeding in captivity. The world's last living quagga, an old female, died in the Amsterdam zoo in 1883.

The Boers also found another species of wild horse in abundance in the Orange Free State and Transvaal—a true zebra with stripes over most of the body but with white legs. They named it bontequagga, or painted quagga, but the English called it Burchell's zebra (*Equus burchelli burchelli*) after the naturalist who described it. Hunted in the same way as the quagga, Burchell's zebra was very rare by 1850, and by the end of the nineteenth century it had disapeared completely in the wild.

Three other races of the same species survive today, although all of them are hard pressed for living space. They include Chapman's zebra (*E. b. antiquorum*), which ranges from the Transvaal to Angola; Grant's zebra (*E. b. bohmi*), which is found from northern Rhodesia to Ethiopia; and Selous's zebra (*E. b. selousi*) of Mozambique, southern Rhodesia, and Nyasaland.

CAPE MOUNTAIN ZEBRA

Equus zebra zebra

Writing nearly two thousand years ago, Roman historian Dio Cassius described zebras picturesquely and splendidly as "horses of the sun which resemble tigers." He was probably speaking of the species we know as Grevy's zebra (*Equus grevyi*), which is found in Ethiopia and the southern Sudan, one part of Africa that the Romans knew a little about because of their exploratory trips up the Nile. Grevy's, with its many narrow stripes, is the largest of the zebras and one of the handsomest. Besides Grevy's zebra and the various races of Burchell's zebra, the third full species of the handsome horses of the sun is the mountain zebra of southern Africa. One race of this species, the Cape Mountain zebra, ranged over the southern parts of Cape Colony when the Dutch first settled there.

Smallest of the zebras, the Cape Mountain zebra is only forty-eight inches high at the shoulder and has very wide black stripes. Like the quagga, it was hunted relentlessly by the settlers. By 1656 it had become so scarce that it was awarded special protection by Jan van Riebeeck, one of the Dutch governors of Cape Province. Linnaeus described the species in 1758. When the British took over the Cape, they relaxed hunting laws, and the Cape Mountain zebra, along with the quagga, quickly dwindled.

By the early years of the twentieth century only several hundred were left, due to hunting pressure, competition from domestic stock, and loss of habitat. Several conservation-minded Boer families saved the Cape Mountain zebra, however, protecting a few small bands of them on their farms.

From this seed stock, six individuals, including one mare, were sent in 1937 to the Cape Mountain Zebra Park, newly established by the Government of South Africa. There were fewer than fifty surviving animals at this time.

With only one mare, this original group of six did not thrive at the park. They had died out by 1950 when eleven new animals with a more equal sex ratio were brought in. Results were more encouraging this time. By 1964 the park had trebled in size with an additional 12,700 acres, and thirty new animals were added to the herd.

Today the total population of the Cape Mountain zebra is still under two hundred. Nearly three fourths of them are at Cape Mountain Zebra National Park, and about a dozen specimens at the DeHoop Nature Reserve. In addition, perhaps three dozen are still free ranging.

A much lighter form of the species, Hartman's Mountain zebra (*Equus z. hartmannae*), has a considerably larger population, but it is also vulnerable. Ranging widely in southwestern Africa and Angola, this subspecies numbered about seven thousand animals in 1970. That total, however, was down more than 50 percent from a population of some fifteen thousand in 1960.

BONTEBOK AND BLESBOK
Damaliscus dorcas dorcas and *D. d. phillipsi*

Many wildlife species besides the quagga and mountain zebra suffered greatly because of the European settlement of South Africa. The earliest victim was a handsome antelope, the blaabok, or bluebuck (*Hippotragus leucophaeus*), which became extinct in 1800. It was the first large African animal to be exterminated by Europeans. The quagga and Cape Mountain zebra followed it into extinction, and many other animals were very nearly wiped out.

Among them were the bontebok and blesbok, two different races of the same species of antelope. The bontebok is a sleek but sturdy animal with lyre-shaped horns. Its color is mainly dark brown, but its face, rump, underparts, and lower part of the legs are white. Its close relative, the blesbok, is a brighter chestnut color and has a pale tan rump patch.

The bontebok was originally found only in a narrow strip of

bontebok

grassland in the southwest section of Cape Province, hemmed in by mountains to the north and by coastal swamps to the south. Settlers moved into this region very early, and the bontebok was soon reduced to perilously low numbers by reckless hunting and the conversion of its natural habitat to agricultural lands and cattle pastures. The surviving bontebok were forced into the narrow coastal strip that was unsuitable for farming. There, in 1864, several conservation-minded farm families took steps to preserve them. One farmer by the name of Van der Byl succeeded in guiding a group of 300 bontebok into a large fenced enclosure on his ranch and protecting them. Several other families took similar measures, and the bontebok was thus saved from extermination.

By 1927—more than sixty years later—there were about 120 bontebok living on seven farms. In 1931, the Government of South Africa established a Bontebok National Park of some 1700 acres in a coastal area east of Capetown and stocked it with 22 of these farm-preserved animals. The animals in the park had increased to about 120 by 1953. But then they started to dwindle—perhaps because the coastal site of the park was not suitable habitat for them—and by 1960 only 72 bontebok survived there.

The Government established a new park that year at Swellendam, further inland, and transplanted 61 bontebok there from the old park; the remaining 11 were taken to wildlife farms. At Swellendam they flourished, and today surplus stock is sent to selected farmers for them to protect on their farms. The total present population is close to 1000 animals. One farmer alone has raised a herd of 200 bontebook in the past thirty years and has sent over half of them to other interested individuals.

The bontebok's close relative, the blesbok, was once common from Cape Province to the Transvaal and Orange Free State, but it became extinct in the wild during the nineteenth century. In the twenty years from 1863 to 1883, hide hunters were said to have slaughtered blesbok by the tens of thousands. A few were preserved by farmers in the same way that the bontebok had been preserved, however, and today the blesbok flourishes on a number of game preserves in the Transvaal and Orange Free State, as well as on numerous farms.

GIANT SABLE ANTELOPE
Hippotragus niger variani

In 1909, the Trans-African Benguela Railroad was being constructed between the Angolan port of Lobito and the copper mines of Rhodesia, some 1300 miles to the east. One of the supervisors of this project was H. F. Varian, an English engineer. A wildlife enthusiast, Varian was especially taken with the magnificent giant sable antelopes that he observed in small herds along the railroad right-of-way. He had never seen sable antelopes like them anywhere.

Standing close to fifty-five inches high at the shoulder and weighing about six hundred pounds, the male giant sable flaunts great crescent-shaped horns that grow up to sixty-five inches in length. The animal's coat is glistening black, with contrasting white facial markings, white belly and buttocks. The somewhat smaller females are a rich golden-chestnut color.

Varian procured the type specimen of the sable antelope in 1913, and the zoologist Oldfield Thomas described it in 1916, last of the large African animals to be officially discovered and scientifically described.

Long before, however, the giant sable had been known as one of the world's most outstanding big-game hunting trophies. Boer immigrants had killed many of these magnificent creatures in the 1870s for their meat, hides, and horns. The hunting was still going on when Varian discovered them, and he was alarmed at its extent. He persuaded officials of the Portuguese Govern-

ment to declare the sable antelope "royal game" so that over much of its range it could be taken only under special permit.

Despite such measures, trophy hunting and poaching of the giant sable continued. In 1939, one African traveler declared that he had ". . . heard several Portuguese brag of killing ten sable a month. At that rate, this magnificent animal will soon be extinct."

Besides the pressure of such illicit hunting, the pressures of an increasing human population were also beginning to encroach upon the giant sables' habitats. The wooded savannahs frequented by the species were invaded by pastoral tribes with herds of cattle, and much of the woodland was cut, cleared, and burned. The big antelopes were forced out, and their population began to decline. By the late 1950s only an estimated five hundred or so were left. But the imposition of a stiff $3500 fine helped to control the poaching.

In 1957, the Angolan Government created 4000-square-mile Luanda Natural Integral Reserve to protect the giant sable. Six years later a second protected area—the Malange Reserve—was created. Today the total population of giant sable antelopes, most of them in these two areas, is estimated at five hundred to two thousand animals.

Poaching is still going on to some extent in spite of the stiff fines, and the cattle-raising peoples still invade the reserves. Moreover, the habitat still deteriorates, and so the population of sables decreases. The fierce fighting that swept across Angola in the winter of 1975 and 1976 no doubt contributed to this reduction.

OKAPI
Okapia johnstoni

In 1899, the High Commissioner for Uganda, Sir Harry Johnston, rescued a group of Pygmies—people of the Belgian Congo's Ituri Forest—from the greedy clutches of a wandering German entrepreneur who planned to exhibit them at the forthcoming 1900 Paris Exposition. The Pygmies lived with Sir Harry for several months before he was able to return them to their forest home, and they became friends. Among other things, they told him about a strange animal that lived in the Ituri Forest, a creature that they called "okapi." From their description, the animal was evidently rather like a mule in shape and was dark colored with contrasting light zebra stripes.

Sir Harry knew of no such animal, but he recalled that Henry Stanley, in his book *In Darkest Africa,* had mentioned a beast that might fit that description. Stanley had written: "The Wambutti knew a donkey and called it 'Atti.' They say that they sometimes catch them in pits."

His curiosity whetted, Sir Harry determined to do his best to track down this unknown beast when he returned the Pygmies to their homeland. Arriving at Fort Mbeni in the Congo Free State, he questioned the Belgian officers there and learned that although they had never seen the animal alive, they knew it through the local hunters who killed it for its delicious meat.

The Belgians promised to get him a complete skin of the animal. Sir Harry wrote to Dr. Sclater of the London Zoological Society on August 21, 1900, telling him what he had learned and stating that he would send samples of skin and other parts as soon as he got them. Two strips of skin, bartered from local hunters, duly arrived, and on the basis of them, Dr. Sclater named the unknown animal *Equus* (?) *johnstoni,* in honor of Sir Harry Johnston. His question mark indicated that he was not certain that this newly described species belonged to the horse family.

Not long thereafter a Swedish officer in the Belgian service, Karl Ericksson, sent Sir Harry a whole skin plus two skulls of the animal. They were sent off to London in June, 1901, and on examining them, Professor Ray Lankester rechristened the animal, giving it the generic name *Okapia.*

The okapi's closest living relative is the giraffe, and the species itself must closely resemble the long-extinct *Samotherium,* which roamed Europe and Asia some fifteen million or more years ago. Male okapis have short, skin-covered horns, and in the case of both sexes the velvety coat is dark chocolate in color, with many contrasting white stripes on the flanks and legs. The animal's head is long and pointed, and the prehensile tongue can be extended to considerable distances to reach out and pull foliage into the mouth.

That an animal as large and distinctive as the okapi was not discovered by scientists until the twentieth century seems remarkable. But the region in which it is found, a 700-by-140-mile strip of tropical rain forest in the northeastern Congo, is one of the world's least explored areas and for good reason. The rain forest of equatorial Africa is almost impenetrable.

"The immensity of wilderness is appalling; for over eighteen hundred miles without a break it stretches more than half way across the continent, from the coast of Guinea to the Ruwenzori. In spite of tropical luxuriance, it is one of the most dismal spots

on the face of the globe, for the torrid sun burns above miles of leafy expanse, and the unflagging heat of about one hundred degrees, day and night, renders the moist atmosphere unbearable. Over the whole area storms of tropical violence thunder and rage almost daily. Here natives have become cannibals, and the graves of thousands of white men are merely a remembrance of where youthful energy and adventure came to a sudden end."

The writer of this passage was Herbert Lang, a zoologist and wild-animal collector, who in 1909 was commissioned by Dr. Henry Fairfield Osborn—then the president of both the American Museum of Natural History and the New York Zoological Society—to head up an expedition to the Congo to collect museum specimens and live animals for both of these institutions. Departing from New York in the spring of 1909 with a young ornithologist at the museum, James P. Chapin, as his sole companion, Lang remained in the Congo until 1915. Okapis were the expedition's most-desired specimens: first, for a habitat group at the museum; and second, if possible, a live animal for the zoo.

Lang was successful in achieving the first objective, for he soon learned that the species was not uncommon within its restricted rain-forest range. The Pygmies, in fact, often hunted it for its meat and hide, and the Bantu tribes trapped the okapi in snares and pitfalls. Local hunters assured Lang that a Mangbetu chief named Zebandra had some years before taken eleven okapis within a week's time by using some eight hundred beaters to drive them into snares, pitfalls, and nets.

But the expedition failed to catch a live okapi, after being within sight of success. A week-old calf was actually captured, and it lived until it had exhausted the stock of canned milk. No substitute food was available, and the little animal soon died. The expedition had to return to New York in 1915 without a live okapi.

The same year, however, another young okapi was captured in the Belgian Congo and successfully reared at a mission station. There it remained until 1919 when World War I ended. The four-year-old specimen was then shipped to the Antwerp Zoo, where it lived only forty days. In 1937, the Bronx Zoo finally got a male okapi. The first of its species ever to be seen in America, it lived at the Bronx Zoo for many years.

Although evidently not uncommon within its wilderness habitat, the okapi has a very restricted range, and its total population during historic times must always have been quite small. Until recent years it has been protected by the remoteness and inaccessibility of its habitat. Unfortunately, such protection diminishes year by year. Roads built by the Belgians now penetrate into the heart of the okapi's home forest.

CONGO PEACOCK, OR AFROPAVO
Afropavo congensis

The 1909-1915 expedition to the Congo failed in its efforts to bring back a live okapi to the New York Zoological Park, but it did bring back a treasure-house of specimens for the American Museum of Natural History. James P. Chapin, Lang's young assistant on that expedition, spent years studying and describing the birds he had brought from the area, and ultimately he became known as the world's leading authority on birds of the Congo region.

For years he puzzled over several feathers he had brought back from that first expedition. These wing quills, which were used by a native of the Congo in a feather headdress, were a warm rusty-red color with many black bars. Chapin had obtained them in the Ituri Forest in 1913, but they did not belong to any bird that he had ever seen in the area. Although they looked like the flight feathers of a pheasant or peafowl, no members of the pheasant family were known in Africa. Chapin set the feathers down as an unsolved mystery.

They remained a puzzle until he went to Belgium in 1936. There, twenty-three years after he had collected them, he found their companions. At the Congo Museum, in Tervueren, near Brussels, he glimpsed a couple of dusty mounted birds atop a cabinet. ". . . never had I seen any like these," he recorded later. "They were somewhat larger than domestic fowls; one appeared blackish, the other more rufous. Yet the black-barred wing feathers of the rufous bird awoke a memory." That memory was of the two puzzling wing quills he had brought home more than twenty years before.

These mounted birds at the Congo Museum were labeled *"Pavo cristatus, jeune, importé"*: Peafowl, young, imported. But when he examined them closely, Chapin quickly realized that they were not Asian peafowl. Checking further, he learned that they, along with a number of other bird specimens, had been donated to the Congo Museum some years earlier by the Kasai Company, a private trade-monopoly concern that controlled a huge southern part of the Congo Free State.

Recognizing that he had a new bird species in hand—indeed they formed a new bird genus, the first new one recognized by ornithologists in over forty years—Chapin named the birds *Afropavo congensis,* Congo peacock. But as yet he had not seen the living bird.

The next week he sat at a reception next to Monsieur de Mathelin de Papigny, a mining engineer from the Congo, who told Chapin of a strange bird he had eaten for dinner some years before when he had been working at a gold mine near Angumu, west of Lake Edward. When he described it, Chapin realized that de Papigny was describing the Congo peafowl. Now, with a specific locality in which to search for the species, he returned to the Congo in June, 1937. Arriving at Stanleyville, he was soon successful in collecting the skins of eight birds, and in July he saw his first living specimen. He learned that the birds traveled in pairs, roosted in trees at night, and emitted loud, nocturnal calls. Although not uncommon in certain localized areas, the species evidently has a very restricted range.

Since their discovery, the Congo peacock has been kept at

several different zoos and has bred successfully in the Antwerp and Rotterdam Zoos.

CHEETAH
Acinonyx jubatus

Crouching on its belly, the lithe spotted cat peers through the tall grass. Ahead, a band of Thomson's gazelles are feeding. Stalking slowly and silently forward on long, lean legs, the cheetah approaches to within a hundred yards of its unsuspecting prey. Then suddenly it bounds forward with great speed. Surprised and confused, the gazelles scatter.

Light as thistledown, the big cat overtakes one of the antelope, brings it down, and quickly kills it. Often considered the world's fastest mammal, the cheetah can move at speeds of sixty miles an hour, more for short distances, enabling it to overtake gazelles and other swift antelopes. Living in an open grassland environment—only 5 percent of Africa below the Sahara Desert is suitable—it hunts by sight and is most active during daylight

hours. Slender and slight of build, it weighs only 120 to 130 pounds, and it has claws that are only partially retractable. It seldom defends its kill if challenged by other predators such as hyenas or Cape hunting dogs.

The cheetah once ranged westward from India across southern Asia and North Africa and southward through the African plains and savannahs to South Africa. Today it has disappeared from much of its African territory and has been exterminated practically everywhere in Asia in spite of its former abundance there.

The name cheetah comes from the Hindi word *chita,* which means "spotted," and Indian rulers once delighted in using their tame captive cheetahs to bring down blackbuck and deer, much as falconers use birds of prey to capture smaller animals. The sixteenth-century Mogul Emperor, Akbar the Great, reportedly kept 1000 trained cheetahs for the hunt.

Today the cheetah is extinct in India; the last one was killed around 1952. A very few may still survive in the Afghanistan-USSR border region, and eastern Iran still harbors perhaps two or three hundred. Elsewhere in Asia the cheetah has been wiped out.

In Africa, the cheetah has fared somewhat better, but it will eventually disappear there also, unless the trend changes. Today there may be ten to twenty thousand African cheetahs left. Most of them survive in East Africa where they are protected in parks such as Serengeti National Park in Tanzania and Kenya's Tsavo.

Through the years the African cheetah has been hunted relentlessly, not only for its beautiful spotted fur but because it is a predator that sometimes preys on domestic stock. Thus, it has been virtually exterminated from ranch country in Kenya, Rhodesia, and South Africa. Even where it is protected, poachers kill it for its handsome spotted hide. As recently as 1968 and

1969, a total of 3168 cheetah skins were imported into the United States.

"In 1960, there were probably twice as many cheetahs as there are now," one investigator states, and he goes on to predict that today's population will be halved in another ten years unless drastic action is taken to protect the species.

LEOPARD
Panthera pardus

One of the most beautiful of all the big cats, the leopard has tawny-yellow fur decorated with dark spots clustered together in rosette shapes. With a wide range, it roams suitable habitat in Asia from the Caucasus to eastern Siberia and southward through India and all of Southeast Asia to Java. It also occurs over much of Africa. Many races of this powerful cat have been described.

Although neither as fast nor as lithe as the cheetah, the leopard is a far stronger animal. A forest dweller, it is an excellent climber and usually hunts at night, often waiting on a tree branch and springing down upon its unsuspecting victim.

At least five different races of leopard have virtually disappeared: the Sinai leopard, which was thought to be extinct until several specimens were seen within the past several years; the Arabian leopard, which is being killed off by shepherds to protect their flocks; the Barbary leopard of Morocco, Algeria, and Tunisia, with an estimated population of only a few hundred animals; the Anatolian leopard of western Asia and Transcaucasia, now very rare; and the Amur leopard of eastern Siberia, which is also in imminent danger of extinction.

Although its overall population has declined in recent years, the leopard is still common in many parts of southern Asia, where a melanistic form—the black leopard—lives. It is fairly common in much of Africa south of the Sahara as well. Legally

protected as a game animal in some countries, it is hunted down as vermin—a danger to man and his domestic stock—in others. And everywhere it is stalked by poachers, who take its handsome spotted hide for the fur trade. During the 1960s, a single poaching center in Ethiopia exported about eight thousand leopard skins annually. Very few big-game species can stand attrition like that for long.

In Kenya's Tsavo National Park, and Tanzania's Serengeti National Park, wildlife biologists are studying leopard habits by trapping them in box traps, temporarily tranquilizing them with drugs, and fitting them with radio collars that contain battery-powered transmitters. The animals are then released. By following the signals transmitted by the collars, biologists are able to map the animals' travels and home ranges. Similar techniques have been used by biologists in the United States for studying mountain lions, as well as grizzly and polar bears.

Relentless hunting—because of the leopard's predator status and because of its valuable fur—is taking its toll of leopard populations everywhere. During recent years the United States has banned importation of leopard skins, and in 1971 members of the International Fur Trade Federation suggested a three-year ban on use of leopard skins until the results of a worldwide survey of the species could be evaluated. This suggestion was merely a recommendation, however, and in 1973 some twenty thousand leopard skins for the fur trade were shipped out of Africa, most of them going to Europe.

Sponsored by the IUCN and the World Wildlife Fund, wildlife biologist Norman Myers recently conducted a two-year survey of African leopard populations. He concluded in 1974 that there were at least one hundred thousand of the handsome spotted beasts still roaming Africa, but that the species was severely reduced in many of its former haunts. Blaming the fur trade for the predicament in which all the big cats find themselves, he recommended that all trade in leopard skins be stopped until a better program and policy could be developed. One such possibility that he suggested was a closely regulated and controlled annual harvest of leopard skins for the fur trade. "Many observers are convinced," said Dr. Myers, "that all wildlife—not just the leopard—will be crowded out from almost every corner of the land unless it can prove its worth in terms of hard cash."

Many other wildlife experts disagreed vehemently with that conclusion. Peter Scott, the eminent English conservationist, countered by observing: "In many cases a legitimate trade opens the floodgates to illegitimate poaching." Meanwhile, the harvest of leopard skins continues, and the question remains of how much longer the species can hold out.

AFRICAN, OR NILE, CROCODILE
Crocodylus niloticus

The mighty Nile sweeps more than four thousand miles from its sources in the heart of Africa to the Mediterranean, bringing life—and sometimes death—to the people who live along it. On its banks lie great reptiles basking in the sun, armored dragons surviving from the age of dinosaurs, hundreds of millions of years ago. Their amber cat eyes gleam with the reflected gold of the sun; their gaping jaws reveal jagged rows of long, sharp teeth. A rugged armor of bronze green covers the squat body and the long saw-toothed tail, all except for the belly, which has yellow leathery plates.

Silently one eighteen-foot monster slides into the water and floats like a submerged log, with only eyes, nostrils, and ears above water. An unwary waterbird drifts toward the log, which moves imperceptibly forward to meet it. One snap, a startled squawk, and the bird disappears. Satisfied for the moment, the crocodile sinks beneath the surface.

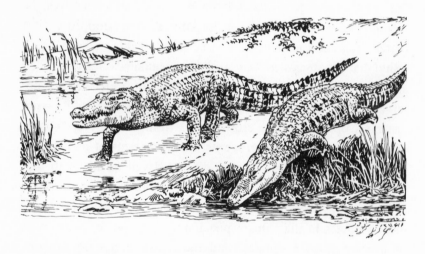

Little changed from the animal that coexisted with the dinosaurs, the Nile crocodile is a fearsome-looking beast. Once abundant on the Nile and most of Africa's other rivers, it has long been feared and persecuted. In ancient times, however, it was held sacred in some areas. Legend has it that Mona, the first King of Egypt, was saved when threatened by wild dogs by jumping onto the back of a crocodile at Lake Moeris, after which the obliging beast carried him to the safety of the opposite bank. To some Egyptians the crocodile was the symbol of Sebek, the water god, who caused the Nile to rise and spread out over the land, fertilizing and irrigating it. Even today the people of Paga in northern Ghana venerate the crocodile. They raise crocodiles in ponds and tame them enough so that children can ride on their backs. The people of Paga believe that each crocodile has within it the spirit of one of their ancestors and that the children are merely playing with their relatives.

But elsewhere in Africa today, the crocodile is feared as a destroyer of game animals and livestock and occasionally of unwary human beings as well. In many areas it is killed as vermin; in others it is hunted for its handsome hide, which has long been in great demand for use in leather products.

David Livingstone and his brother observed a lot of crocodile hunting in their travels. More than a century ago they recorded: "Crocodiles in the Rovuma [a river which forms the present boundary between Tanzania and Mozambique] have a sorry time of it. Never before were reptiles so persecuted and snubbed. They are hunted with spears, and spring traps are set for them. If one enters an inviting pool after fish, he soon finds a fence thrown around it, and a spring trap set in the only path out of the enclosure. Their flesh is eaten and relished. The banks, on which the female lays her eggs at night, are carefully searched by day, and all the eggs are dug out and devoured. The fish-hawk makes havoc among the few that escape their other enemies."

Crocodiles were abundant throughout Africa's waterways during Livingstone's time, and in many areas they remained common until a few years ago. But now, after years of relentless killing, the species is disappearing everywhere. It has been completely exterminated in Egypt and along the lower Nile in recent years, and it is in difficulty in East Africa. Traditional crocodile breeding grounds in countless areas are being destroyed by the pressures of human settlement: the clearing and altering of stream banks, drainage projects, sewage, and pollution.

Poaching has also been a principal cause of the crocodile's downfall. Philip Crowe, in his 1971 book, *World Wildlife, the Last Stand,* tells of one poacher, Bobbie Wilmot, who worked the Kalahari region and the Chobe River area between southern Zaire and Bechuanaland. "Wilmot's main business is still hunting crocodiles," he relates. "Since he started crocodile hunting in 1954, he has killed about 42,000 of them and of late years has averaged 2,000 skins a year. These are worth about twenty-five dollars for a prime skin. In the future, however, he is going to run a crocodile farm where he will raise his own stock." Such farming is already being practiced to some extent in Asia with the Thai crocodile, and in North America with the alligator. In the end, such farms could be the possible preserver of all the species of crocodilians, as long as poaching still exists and the use of the hides is still legal.

As it is, all crocodilians are threatened because of the continuing demand for their skins. Many authorities believe that their only hope for survival lies in making international agreements that would prohibit the importation of skins into Europe, the United States, and other centers of the hide industry. New York State's Mason Act, for example, prohibits the importation of any such hides into New York State and City, the latter an industry center. Representatives of the industry maintain that controls should be applied at the source, with sufficient numbers of wardens to prevent poaching so that only legal hides could be sold on the market. In practice, however, the areas to be patrolled are too vast, and poachers can easily elude the wardens.

Murchison Falls National Park supports the last relatively undisturbed crocodile population in Uganda and is one of the few places on the Nile River where the species still occurs to any extent. An English zoologist, Dr. Hugh Cott, has conducted various surveys of the crocodiles in this area over a period of years. Cott reports that in 1952 ". . . one of the most spectacular congregations of crocodiles to be found anywhere on the Victoria Nile was at the Mugunga grounds. There one could see a compact formation of reptiles so numerous that when disturbed it looked as though the whole beach was moving into the river. This congregation was still present in strength in 1957. Four years later the place was deserted. . . . The nesting population below Paraa has now been virtually exterminated by skin hunters."

In a 1968 report, he noted that crocodiles were being poached from the park at a rate of 20 per month. Unless such poaching was quickly checked, he believed that the last stand of crocodiles in Uganda would be destroyed within a few years. The estimated crocodile population below Murchison Falls in 1967 was 700, with no more than 250 nesting females. In 1972, another survey showed a total population of only 241 animals.

Dr. Cott learned that the disturbance of nesting females in the park by tourist motor launches was having a fatally damaging effect on both the eggs and young. The female crocodile digs a hole in the sandy shore and lays a clutch of as many as fifty eggs in January or February. Covering the nest, she remains close by for three months, guarding the eggs until they hatch. As they hatch out of the eggs, the young grunt, a signal to the mother to uncover them, which she does. Leading or carrying her offspring to shallow water, she continues to watch over them for six weeks or more until they have a reasonable chance of survival on their own.

When a boat comes too close, which may happen as many as a dozen times a day, the female crocodile abandons her nest area or her young. With the mother absent, predators quickly move in and devour the eggs or young. Some common predators are the big Goliath heron and the marabou stork, both of which probe for the eggs with their long beaks and also gulp down the young whole. Fish eagles, kites, and monitor lizards prey on them too, as do such mammalian predators as baboons, hyenas, and honey badgers. More than half of the recent nests and eggs in the Murchison Falls area have been destroyed by such enemies when the mother crocodile is driven away.

One possible answer to such destruction of crocodiles is an experimental program being conducted in South Africa's Mkuzi Game Preserve. Eggs are collected from nests of wild crocodiles, placed in damp grass inside boxes, and artificially incubated at temperatures between 80 and 95 degrees Fahrenheit. When the young hatch, they are cared for in pens until they are old enough to be released in selected areas chosen for restocking.

Alarmed about the rapid downward trend of crocodilian populations all over the world—some twenty species in all—the Crocodile Specialist group of IUCN's Survival Service met in 1973 at Ndumu and St. Lucia Game Reserves in Zululand. There they worked out a program aimed at saving nine threatened species of crocodilians—including the Nile crocodile—throughout the world and helping to preserve all of them. The program includes surveys of wild populations and the principal hide sources, special legal action to help species on the verge of extinction, the promotion of adequate sanctuaries, and a worldwide publicity campaign aimed at focusing attention on crocodilian ecology and the benefits these reptiles exert on their surroundings. They help to control predatory fish, for example, which feed on desirable food fish, and a number of species dig deep water holes, which in times of drought are vital for many different kinds of wildlife.

Meanwhile, the issue of crocodile hunting and poaching is still being debated. Should legal and controlled hunting be permitted, and should crocodilians be farmed as a valuable source of fine leather? Or should a worldwide ban be established on all traffic and use of crocodilian skins? The future of the Nile crocodile, and all other crocodilians, hinges on the manner in which these questions are answered.

The Future of Africa's Wildlife

What lies in store for the wildlife of Africa depends very much upon which of various conflicting attitudes and policies will eventually prevail. They are still in flux, and time grows very short. Conservationists say that at least sixty species of mammals south of the Sahara, and an even greater number of other forms of wildlife, are presently in danger; year by year the total grows. One observer voices the common concern: "Hemmed in by rising human populations, harassed by poachers, stalked by hunters and tourist hordes—Africa's wildlife faces at best an uncertain coexistence with man on a continent full of hungry mouths."

Human population in Africa is increasing at a rate of 3 to 4 percent yearly, a doubling of the total population every twenty-eight or thirty years. And the populations of man's domestic flocks increase at about twice that rate. The rising tide of humanity needs more land for crops, more land for grazing animals, more land for industry and development. All over the continent forests are being cut, grasslands fenced and plowed or overgrazed, and wildlife destroyed when it competes with cattle for food. And poaching continues to take an appalling toll of the continent's wildlife. As a result, Africa today has perhaps one tenth of the wildlife population that it supported in 1900.

At that time Africa was still a paradise for hunters, in spite of centuries of slaughter. First to be exploited was the wildlife of North Africa, which started its decline some two thousand years ago in Roman times. In South Africa the killing began in the seventeenth century, and there whole wildlife populations were slaughtered in the same ruthless manner that the bison was later exterminated in most of North America.

Africa's heartland, the tropical rainforests and the rugged country of the middle of the continent, remained relatively unexploited until the twentieth century, because of the difficulties in penetrating the vast stretches of forest and also because of the dangers posed by the tsetse fly and other disease-carrying pests. During the past thirty or forty years, however, these difficulties have been conquered to some extent, and now the exploitation of both land and wildlife is well under way there too.

At Jinja, Uganda—the remote spot where Captain John Speke discovered the spectacular Ripon Falls in 1862, and where the Nile starts its 4000-mile sweep to the Mediterranean—there is no Ripon Falls today. Instead, there is a huge hydroelectric dam. Uganda is striving mightily to develop its land and its economy. During the past forty-five years it has converted more than 70 percent of its wild land to agriculture and killed countless thousands of its game animals in programs aimed at controlling the tsetse fly. Neighboring Rhodesia killed nearly a half million big-game animals in twenty-five years for the same reason.

On the northern rim of the continent the Sahara advances steadily, creeping relentlessly into neighboring savannah and bush country. The desert-making process is hastened by overgrazing by domestic animals, and the attempts of pastoral tribes to raise crops on land not suited for tilling. Such practices, heightened by extended periods of drought, have brought famine and death to untold thousands of people and their domestic animals during the past few years alone. Under such conditions, what hope does the future hold for either wildlife or people in Africa? One approach being tried by Algeria is a twenty-year program of tree planting—similar to that carried out in the United States' dust bowl in the 1930s—to halt the northward advance of the desert. When completed, nearly six billion pines and eucalyptus trees will have been planted in a green belt nearly one thousand miles long and ten miles wide.

Many other African nations have taken positive steps aimed at safeguarding their wildlife heritage. A number of game preserves and national parks have been established, and most of the governments have instituted active antipoaching programs. Many African leaders promote parks and wildlife preserves enthusiastically, for they realize that Africa's spectacular wildlife is one of the continent's most valuable natural resources, a prime attraction for tourists and their dollars. These same leaders are beginning to realize that wildlife could be an important source of food for their hungry people if it could be managed and harvested as the saiga antelope is in Russia or the white-tailed deer in the United States.

The great majority of Africans, however, usually view the matter quite differently, as has been observed by Dr. Mary Jean Aerni, an anthropologist who has worked in Uganda. She states— and many other Europeans on the scene agree—that the parks are not thought of as national treasures or wildlife sanctuaries by the Africans. They think that the parks were established *by* Europeans *for* Europeans and that they are an intrusion on traditional hunting grounds, established for the benefit of foreign tourism with which the local people have very little contact. Furthermore, farmers and herdsmen understandably do not want elephants or rhinos invading their croplands or herds of wild hoofed stock competing with their domestic animals for grass and water.

The East African plains have long been a center of conflicting interests between stock raisers and wildlife conservationists. This whole rich region—especially Tanzania's Serengeti Plain— is blessed with the most spectacular wild-animal herds left on earth. Thousands of wildebeest, zebra, hartebeest, and gazelles, as well as plentiful populations of rhinos, giraffes, lions, leopards, and hyenas roam the grassy plains. The region is also the home-land of the cattle-raising Masai and other pastoral tribes. Much of the area has been taken for the raising of domestic stock at the expense of wildlife since the 1940s. As naturalist Leslie Brown laments: "A unique biological asset that existed nowhere else in the world has been replaced by beef, mutton, and wool, which can be produced in a hundred other places."

Some years ago 5000 square miles of this unique habitat was set aside as the Serengeti National Park, it is true, but under the pressures of livestock raisers, the Tanzanian Government in 1972 opened up a 700-square-mile portion of the park for grazing and development. Poachers are responsible for illegally killing an es-timated 40,000 game animals in and around Serengeti every year. In neighboring Zambia, estimates of the illegal kills run as high as 200,000 victims a year. The poaching toll is staggering in country after country. Unless the present conflicting policies are resolved soon, practically all of the big-game species—hoofed stock and predators alike—face ultimate extermination.

Arguments about the best way to preserve African wildlife are still being vigorously debated. Some wildlife professionals believe that the only way to eliminate poaching is to legalize and strictly control the taking of wildlife for their meat, hides, and other products. They claim that this policy would eliminate the huge profits that poachers enjoy. If the penalties for violations are made tough enough, they argue, the rewards of illegal hunting would not be worth the risk. Others violently disagree with this proposition, saying that such regulations could not and would not be enforced, and there would be little control over the killing.

Still another group believes that Africa's wildlife should be strictly managed, with surplus stock being harvested yearly to feed hungry people. Under management, they say, Africa's game animals could provide a continuous supply of protein and other products at a cheaper cost than domestic livestock, which are not as well adapted to marginal lands nor as disease-resistant as native wild animals. If wildlife is not made a paying proposition, they declare, it will ultimately be exterminated and the land put to other uses. A wildlife management program of this type, aimed at harvesting the game animals of Masailand and selling the meat to the public, has recently been established in Kenya.

A somewhat different approach is advocated by those who say that many different wild species can be preserved by keeping them on farms in semidomestication, as the blesbok and bontebok were preserved a century ago. The African Wildlife Leadership Foundation of Kenya advocates this policy and is presently experimenting with the keeping of several species of antelopes in this manner.

The fate of Africa's wildlife is still undecided. Its future will be determined by the extent to which such programs are implemented and their degree of success. And the will to implement those programs is still very much in doubt. "That is the agonizing problem in Africa, to balance the needs of an emerging people against those of a vanishing wilderness," zoologist Archie Carr has observed. "Wherever human welfare is clearly at stake, everything else has to be sacrificed."

. . . Madagascar has beckoned to natural scientists for over 200 years with its infinite variety of archaic forms of life, the still living fossils of 40 and 50 million years ago.   Edward Steele

5

MADAGASGAR AND
ISLANDS OF THE INDIAN OCEAN

Almost 1,000 miles long and from 200 to 300 miles wide, Madagascar is—after Greenland, New Guinea, and Borneo—the world's fourth largest island. Separated from Africa by the 250-mile-wide Mozambique Channel, it has been isolated from its huge continental neighbor for sixty million years or more. Because of this long isolation without competition from more advanced forms, its evolving plants and animals have developed forms unlike those found anywhere else in the world. As a result, Madagascar has sometimes been called a Noah's ark of ecological riches.

Mankind did not find this lost world and settle on it until the third or fourth century A.D., fifteen hundred years ago. The

first settlers were not Africans, as one might expect, but people
of Malaysian stock who left their home islands somewhere in the
East Indies in search of new living space. Their graceful outrigger canoes sailed across the Indian Ocean before the prevailing tradewinds, perhaps hopping from island to island in the
same way that the Polynesians fanned east and south through
the Pacific to colonize the South Sea islands. Eventually the

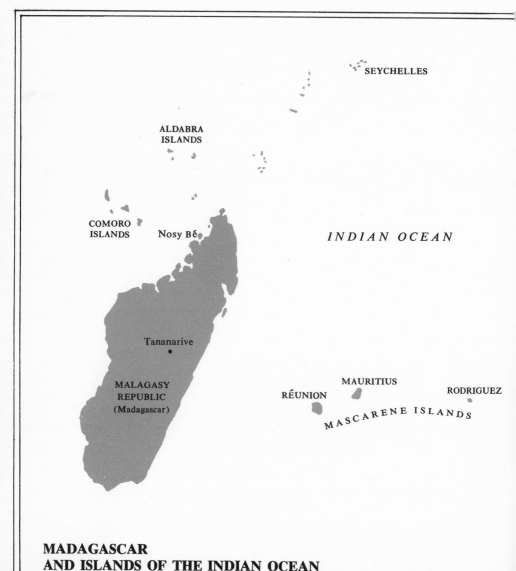

SEYCHELLES

ALDABRA
ISLANDS

COMORO
ISLANDS   Nosy Bé

INDIAN OCEAN

Tananarive

MALAGASY
REPUBLIC
(Madagascar)

MAURITIUS

RÉUNION   RODRIGUEZ

MASCARENE ISLANDS

**MADAGASCAR
AND ISLANDS OF THE INDIAN OCEAN**

pioneering adventurers from the East Indies came to the great island of Madagascar.

Man Changes the Face of the Land

When these early settlers first arrived, Madagascar's eastern highlands, blessed with abundant rainfall, were clad with lush evergreen forests, while the western coastal areas facing Africa had a cover of deciduous forests and wide, grassy savannahs. Its climate was on the whole tropical, with a warm, rainy season from November to April and a drier, cooler season the rest of the year. Most of the center of the island was high plateau, mixed forest, and grassland, with scattered peaks to 9000 feet in altitude. Today the face of the land has been greatly changed. Most of the original forests have been cut, and the grasslands have been modified by repeated burning, overgrazing, and consequent erosion.

Spreading over their new homeland, the people began to clear the land and raise crops and livestock. They were divided into a number of different tribes and kingdoms, and they often warred with one another. As the centuries went by, Arabs and Africans also came to Madagascar, and the island's people became a racial mixture. The language, customs, and flavor of the East Indies, however, remained dominant.

The first European to discover Madagascar was a Portuguese sea captain, Diégo Diaz, who came upon it in 1500 on a voyage of exploration around Africa, searching for a route to the fabled East Indies. French, Dutch, and English explorers followed in the wake of the Portuguese, and a number of smaller Indian Ocean islands were soon discovered as well.

Among them were three volcanic islands lying some 500 to 900 miles east of Madagascar—Réunion, Mauritius, and Rodriguez. Collectively they were known as the Mascarene Islands, after Pedro Mascarenes, a Portuguese mariner who sighted the first two in 1513 as he sailed past them on his way to India. These islands were the home of the extinct dodo bird and its relatives.

About 250 miles north of Madagascar lies the Aldabra Atoll —three small islands surrounding a central lagoon. The main island, just 20 miles long, is the natural home of the only giant tortoises that survive in the Indian Ocean islands today. A related but different tortoise is found on Madagascar.

Some 200 miles south of Aldabra lie the Comoro Islands, a volcanic group consisting of four main islands in the Mozambique Channel, about halfway between Madagascar and the African mainland. In the coastal waters of these islands living specimens of the coelacanth—a fish thought to be extinct for seventy million years or more—were taken by local fishermen on several different occasions during the past twenty years.

Soon after the discovery of Madagascar by Europeans, trading settlements began to appear along its coasts. During the nineteenth century the French became dominant, establishing a protectorate over Madagascar in 1888 and later proclaiming the island a French colony in 1896. This protectorate was supplanted in 1960 by peaceful transition to a republic, with the French still retaining financial control. In 1972, it too was reverted to the people, who now control their own destiny as the Malagasy Republic.

Madagascar's Unique Plants and Animals

The early Europeans in Madagascar and the islands of the Indian Ocean marveled at the many strange plants and animals that were unlike those found anywhere else in the world. On the Mascarenes they discovered the unique flightless birds, the dodo and solitaire. Every island they visited also had its unique population of giant tortoise.

The huge island of Madagascar, however, boasted the

greatest variety of peculiar forms of wildlife. Among these animals were the many species of lemurs—a group of primitive primates that evolved and specialized in many directions during Madagascar's long isolation from Africa. The lemurs' closest relatives are the galagos and bushbabies of Africa and the lorises of Southeast Asia.

Another group of mammals that evolved in isolation into a bewildering variety of specialized forms were the tenrecs—small, primitive insectivores. The only native predatory mammals were a few meat eaters of the family Viverridae. Largest was the fossa, a sleek catlike animal with dark chocolate-black fur and a long tail.

Of the birds, an estimated 65 percent of the two hundred or so breeding species are found nowhere else in the world. Madagascar is also the home of three fourths of the known species of chameleons. Strange as the living animals of Madagascar are today, some that have disappeared, like the elephant bird, were even more striking.

ELEPHANT BIRD, OR AEPYORNIS
Aepyornis maximus

One of the best-known stories of *The Arabian Nights* is the tale of Sinbad, an Arab sailor who was seized in the talons of a giant bird, the Roc, or Rukh, and transported to a fabled island. The idea for this tall tale may very well have come from Madagascar. Arab ships and sailors had been touching on the island since the early Middle Ages at least—probably long before—and natives had told them of a giant bird that lived there.

Marco Polo had certainly heard some version of the giant-bird story, for he relates in his *Book* that in islands south of Zanzibar ". . . is found the bird *Griffin,* which appears there at certain seasons. . . . It was for all the world like an eagle, but one indeed of enormous size; so big in fact that its wings covered

an extent of thirty paces, and its quills were twelve paces long, and thick in proportion. And it is so strong that it will seize an elephant in its talons and carry him high in the air. . . . The people of those isles call the bird *Roc,* and it has no other name."

The first French governor of Madagascar, Admiral Étienne de Flacourt, heard about a giant bird too, but he was more down-to-earth in his mention of it. In his *Histoire de la Grande Isle de Madagascar,* published in 1658, de Flacourt mentions what islanders called the *vouron-patra,* "a giant bird that lays eggs as big as those of an ostrich. . . . The people keep water in the eggs of the vouron-patra." From the way he mentioned the bird, it was evidently still living at that time, although he did not claim to have seen one. Later visitors to Madagascar were told that the eggs were much bigger than ostrich eggs, a fact that was finally substantiated when actual eggs were brought forth and examined.

In 1850, a French seaman, Captain Abadie, secured three such eggs and a number of bones of the giant bird and sent them to Paris. After studying them intensively, the zoologist Geoffroy

Saint Hilaire described the elephant bird scientifically and gave it the name *Aepyornis maximus,* literally "largest of the tall birds."

The elephant bird stood between nine and ten feet in height and weighed in the neighborhood of one thousand pounds—more than three times the weight of the largest bird living today, the African ostrich. The elephant bird had very thick and trunk-like legs with three toes, all of them directed forward. The legs were rather short and supported so much weight that *Aepyornis* could not have been a fast runner. Its eggs sometimes measured close to fifteen inches in length and twelve inches in diameter, and they had a liquid capacity of nearly two gallons.

Aepyornis is thought to have survived until the mid-1600s. Man evidently killed it off not only by hunting it and taking its eggs, but by destroying much of the forest habitat in which it lived.

The largest elephant bird was *Aepyornis maximus,* but at least six other related species—differing mainly in size and weight—have been described from skeletal remains.

MADAGASCAR'S LEMURS
Families Lemuridae, Indridae, and Daubentoniidae

Primitive but specialized primates, some of them probably very much like our remotest ancestors, lemurs evolved in Madagascar during the sixty million or more years of that island's isolation from Africa. The isolation was so long, as one lemur expert puts it, that "whole families evolved rather than just species." Systematists classify them in three families, with a number of different subgroups or genera. All in all, about twenty different species of lemurs survive in Madagascar today. Probably that many or more, judging from the record, have become extinct during the past few centuries. One of these, *Megaladapis,* was almost as big as a gorilla.

Of living lemurs, the family Lemuridae includes the pygmy, dwarf, and mouse lemurs, as well as many common lemurs. The mouse lemurs are the smallest members of the family; some of them have a body only five inches long and are barely larger than many mice. The hairy-eared mouse lemur, discovered in 1875, was thought to be extinct for many years until surviving specimens were rediscovered in 1966. The so-called common lemurs are arboreal and nocturnal animals, most of them squirrel- or cat-sized. Many of them have neck and cheek ruffs and strikingly patterned coats of contrasting colors.

The second family, the Indridae, includes species with such picturesque common names as sifaka, avahi, or woolly lemur, and indri. Sifakas have foxlike faces and long, bushy tails. They get their name from a hiccuplike belch of contentment—*see-fah*—uttered after an ample and satisfying meal. The avahis have dense fleecelike hair, giving them the alternate name of woolly lemur.

Largest of all living lemurs, the indri stands about three feet high when walking on its hind feet, as it sometimes does. Almost

indri

tailless, it has a mostly black-and-white coat. All four of its lateral toes are joined together by a weblike membrane, and they work together in opposition to the first toe. The animal gets its name because the first naturalists who studied the species thought that indri was the native name for it. Pointing to the animal, a local guide would cry, "Indri!" In the Malagasy language, however, the word means "look." The people themselves call the species *babakota,* which means "little old man."

Strange as the indri's appearance may be, its call or song is even more unusual. The writer Faith McNulty describes its effect upon her: "Suddenly the strangest, most thrilling music I have ever heard rose from the hills around us. . . . It was a chorus of high voices, not shrill, but silvery, that rose and fell through a series of liquid notes. . . . It was alien and wild. It was a sound echoing from the distant past. Millions of years ago, indri had greeted the dawn of a young world with a song like this."

The third lemur family, the Daubentoniidae, has only one living species, the aye-aye, which is so different from all other lemurs that it stands in a family by itself.

All the surviving lemurs are threatened with extinction, partly because of hunting but even more because of habitat destruction. The original forests of Madagascar are 90 percent gone, a percentage greater than that for any of the more densely populated European countries. According to some estimates, nearly 70 percent of the island's flora and fauna have already disappeared because of such destruction. The IUCN *Red Data Book* of endangered species currently lists eight different kinds of lemurs in immediate danger of extinction, plus a number of others that are in the vulnerable category. The likelihood is that most of them will disappear before the end of this century unless definite steps are immediately taken to preserve them. More reserves and stricter protective laws are needed as well as a halt to the wholesale destruction of what remains of the natural environment.

Scientists recognize the deadly peril that the lemurs face and are trying in various ways to help them. Probably the world's leading lemurologist is Dr. Jean Jacques Petter, who has studied lemurs in the field for many years and continues his research on captive specimens in laboratories maintained by the French National Museum near Paris. Another lemur research facility is the Oregon Regional Primate Center in Beaverton, Oregon. By far the largest collection of captive lemurs kept for study purposes, however, is housed at Duke University's Field Station for Animal Behavior in North Carolina. At this flourishing station, Dr. Peter Klopfer, the director, supervises research on a lemur collection that recently included some two hundred individuals of fourteen different species.

In Madagascar, lemur protection comes under the jurisdiction of the Department of Waters and Forests, which has supervision and management over a dozen or more reserves that have been set aside for wildlife and plant protection. Several of these reserves are situated on coastal islands, one of them the beautiful little island of Nosy Bé off the northwest coast. The main job of the Department, however, is not lemur protection but the management and cutting of Madagascar's remaining forests for economic gain. Most of the reserves are small areas of natural habitat surrounded by land that is being exploited for grazing or forestry. Pressures to exploit the reserves increase each year.

Many years ago the mongoose lemur and the brown lemur were introduced into the Comoro Islands, approximately three hundred miles north and west of Madagascar, and these two species flourish there today.

Year by year Madagascar becomes a more hazardous habitat for lemurs and other unique wildlife as more and more of the pitiful remnant of original habitat is destroyed by lumbering or burned over for planting crops.

"It is neither sentimental nor exaggerated to say that lemurs are a unique treasure of the living world," states Faith McNulty, after a recent visit to Madagascar. "It is therefore no small tragedy that the extinction of the wild lemurs is at hand. The forests that shelter them are going up in smoke."

AYE-AYE
Daubentonia madagascariensis

In 1780, a French traveler named Sonnerat saw an animal in Madagascar unlike any he had ever seen before. No European zoologist had yet seen one either. About the size of a large cat, the creature had a long bushy tail, huge ears, and round yellow eyes rimmed with black. It had a flat nail on each big toe, and the front feet were equipped with remarkably long and slender fingers. The middle finger of each hand was especially long and thin, ending in a claw curved like a fishhook. Besides these peculiarities, it also had incisor teeth that never stopped growing, similar to those of a rodent. "It has been described," says one zoologist, "as having the teeth of a rabbit, the ears of a bat, the

fur of a wild boar, the hands of a monkey, and the tail of a fox."
This remarkable beast was and is known as the aye-aye. In the
Malagasy language, *Hay! hay!* is an exclamation of surprise; the
animal's alarm call sounds much the same. These utterances are
probably the source of the animal's common name.

The noted French zoologist Baron Cuvier received a specimen of the aye-aye in 1800 and, on the basis of its rodentlike
teeth, classified it as a squirrel. A second zoologist said it was a
peculiar kind of tarsier, and a third simply called it a rodent.
Not until 1863 did an English zoologist named Richard Owen
convince himself and others that the aye-aye was a highly specialized and peculiar type of lemur.

The natural range of the aye-aye formerly included most of
the forests of northeastern and northwestern Madagascar, but
today it has disappeared nearly everywhere. Almost totally arboreal, it builds tree nests in which it rests during the day. At
night it comes out to eat insect grubs and fruit. Superstitious
people have long regarded it as a harbinger of death. Some believe it is the spirit of a man cursed for violating a taboo. Saddled
as it is with such a reputation, the islanders have understandably
kept their distance from the aye-aye. Its numbers, nevertheless,
have dwindled steadily because of the perennial destruction of
more and more of its vitally needed forest habitat. Never common, the aye-aye disappeared almost completely during the
1930s and 1940s, and by the end of World War II it was considered extinct.

In 1957, however, Dr. Jean Jacques Petter discovered a
small relict population of aye-ayes on Madagascar's east coast.
At his suggestion, the Government set aside a reserve for them
at Mahambo, where they had been rediscovered. Aided by a
grant from the World Wildlife Fund, Dr. Petter studied the
behavior of the aye-aye at night with an infrared telescope and
observed how it obtains food. Finding a limb that is a likely

source, the aye-aye taps on it with its long middle finger. Then it presses its huge ear close to the wood and listens. If it hears activity within the limb, it chews a hole through the bark and wood with its rodentlike teeth. Then it slips its slender middle finger into the hole, pulls out the grub with its curved claw, and eats it.

In 1965, Petter persuaded the Government to set aside the two-square-mile island of Nosy Mangabé, off the northeast coast, as an aye-aye sanctuary. After a great deal of effort, nine aye-ayes were captured on the mainland, taken to Nosy Mangabé in 1967, and released. Several others were added later.

The government of the island has recently barred most foreign scientists from field research in Madagascar, except in very special cases. As a result, the fate of the dozen or so aye-ayes released on Nosy Mangabé is not known. The future of this unique species hangs on the slenderest of threads. According to best current estimates, no more than fifty of them survive anywhere.

DODO
Raphus cucullatus and its relatives

Arab sailors had undoubtedly visited Mauritius and Réunion long before their discovery by Europeans, but neither they nor the Portuguese paid them much attention. Small and remote, they remained uninhabited specks of land in the vast ocean until 1598, when Dutch Admiral Jacob Corneliszoon van Neck landed on Mauritius and conducted a preliminary exploration of the island. His crewmen marveled at the giant tortoises and strange birds they saw. One chronicler of the expedition recorded: ". . . there are large birds, as big as our swans, but with bigger heads." They were dodos, clumsy birds with stubby flightless wings, thick legs, and great hooked beaks up to nine inches long. Slate-gray in color, they weighed as much as fifty pounds apiece. The Dutch

called them *walghvogels*—"nauseous or disgusting birds"—because according to some tastes they were evidently not very good to eat. But there were others who claimed that the bird's breast meat was delicious.

Even though opinions varied as to the dodo's edibility, every passing ship stocked up on the birds, killing and salting them, and storing them aboard as a welcome change from the usual shipboard fare. One seaman, Willem Ysbrandtz, wrote in his journal: "We found there also a quantity of geese, pigeons, grey parrots and other sorts of birds, numbers of tortoises, of which there were sometimes twenty-five under the shade of a tree. We took all these animals as many as we wanted, for they did not run away. There were also some dodos, who had small wings and could not fly. They are so fat that they could hardly move. . . ."

Meantime, settlers came to Mauritius, bringing with them pigs, rats, dogs, monkeys, and other exotic species. These animals, together with man himself, sealed the doom of the clumsy, flightless dodos, which nested on the ground and were defenseless against such enemies. As early as 1634, an official of the British East India Company visited Mauritius and noted that he had seen "Dodoes, a strange kind of fowle, twice as big as a

Goose, that can neither flye nor swymm, being Cloven footed." In 1638, just four years later, when he visited the island again, he observed: "We now mett with None."

Once started, the dodo's downfall was swift and complete, and the year 1681 marks the date when the last one was seen alive on Mauritius. The dodo had the unfortunate distinction of being the first documented wildlife species to disappear as the direct result of man's activities. Ever since, the dodo has been a symbol of extinction, as the phrase "dead as a dodo" bears witness. And the year 1681 is used by wildlife conservationists today as the reckoning date from which the tragic and ever-lengthening list of animals exterminated at the hands of modern man is recorded.

A similar bird, the white dodo, lived on Réunion. It was much like its Mauritius relative but a lighter color. It evidently became extinct about 1750, although its actual demise was not noted until 1801, when a scientific survey of the island's animals failed to uncover it.

On remote Rodriguez there was another large flightless bird, the Rodriguez solitaire, as described by a fugitive French Huguenot, François Lequat, who lived on Rodriguez from 1690 to 1692. He published his travel journal in 1708, noting: "Of all the Birds in the Island, the most Remarkable is that which goes by the Name of the Solitary, because 'tis very seldom seen in Company, tho' there are abundance of them." This species disappeared sometime during the eighteenth century.

"A craving for the impossible gratification of seeing, touching or hefting the sheltered, innocent bulk of a dodo comes over me strongly in my more whimsied moments," confesses zoologist Archie Carr. "I suspect it must come over every man with any time to think. I believe our descendants will have more time of that kind. I know they will have a lot more dodos than we have, to yearn to have been allowed to see."

MAURITIUS KESTREL
Falco punctatus

This attractive little falcon, with spotted white breast and striped tail, looks somewhat like the American kestrel, or sparrow hawk. Its closest relatives, however, are the Madagascar kestrel and the somewhat larger African species. Found only on the island it is named for, the Mauritius kestrel was a common species a century ago. Gradually it became rarer through the years, partly as a result of the destruction of its natural habitat through forestry and cultivation. The introduction of exotic animals such as the rat, cat, mongoose, and monkey—all of which prey on the eggs and young—also contributed to its downfall. The human inhabitants of Mauritius constantly persecuted the species too. They knew the little falcon as *mangeur de poule,* "chicken eater," and killed it whenever they had the chance.

By the mid-1960s the Mauritius kestrel was one of the world's rarest birds, with an estimated ten pairs surviving. In the early 1970s, in an effort to save the species, the World Wildlife Fund, the New York Zoological Society, and the International Council of Bird Preservation organized a Mauritius kestrel survival project and sent Dr. Stanley Temple, an ornithologist at

Cornell University, to Mauritius to see what could be done. In 1973, he and his wife caught a pair of the birds and took them to Cornell University's Laboratory of Ornithology, where they organized an effort to breed them in captivity. A successful program of breeding American peregrine falcons had already been carried through at the same laboratory. Returning to Mauritius the following year, Dr. Temple noted that according to his best estimates, no more than five free-flying wild birds survived on the island—two pairs and one unmated individual.

Later he reported moderately encouraging news from both the wild birds and the captive pair at Cornell. One pair of the island kestrels had nested in a hole on a cliff in Black River Gorge, where the eggs were reasonably safe from monkeys and rats. At least two fledglings had survived. This nesting was evidently the first successful one on Mauritius in two years.

Meanwhile, the captive pair at Cornell had mated and the female laid two eggs. But only one of the eggs proved fertile. It hatched in October, but the infant falcon died when the incubator in which it had been placed suffered a rare malfunction. The adult pair, however, began to show signs of nesting again. If the Temples do succeed in raising Mauritius kestrels in captivity, they hope to be able to release some of them in protected reserves on the island.

ALDABRAN GIANT TORTOISE
Testudo gigantea

The little Aldabra Atoll is the last home and breeding grounds of a unique reptile—the Aldabran giant tortoise. The nearest surviving relatives of these huge, dignified beasts are the giant land tortoises of the Galapagos Islands, located some six hundred miles off the coast of Ecuador, on the other side of the world. Several million years ago, however, giant tortoises were evidently widely distributed over many continents and islands.

As recently as a few centuries ago, distinct forms of these reptiles could be found in South America, the Galapagos Islands, Madagascar, the Mascarenes, and on other islands of the Indian Ocean as well, often in great abundance. They all belonged to the genus *Testudo,* with several different species found on different island groups.

Visiting Rodriguez in 1691, François Lequat reported: " . . . such a plenty of land turtles in this isle that sometimes you see two or three thousand of them in a flock, so that you may go above a hundred paces on their backs." Yet, as a result of ruthless slaughter, the Rodriguez tortoises were all gone by 1786, less than a century later. Records show that in just one eighteen-month period, ships' crews took about thirty thousand of the huge beasts from the island for fresh meat as a welcome change from their typical diet at sea. The tortoises of Mauritius, Réunion, and the Seychelles were exploited in similar fashion. As a result of such practice, the giant tortoises have long since been exterminated everywhere except for those that live and breed on Aldabra and a few captive specimens.

Portuguese seamen first visited the Aldabra Atoll in 1511, and until about a century ago ships made frequent stops at the islands to capture giant tortoises and take them aboard as fresh meat for long ocean voyages to the Far East. Charles Darwin, the celebrated British evolutionist, had been fascinated to see the giant tortoises of the Galapagos in 1835. When there was a movement afoot in 1874 to exploit Aldabra's mangrove timber, he rose to the defense of these other tortoise islands and led a movement to set Aldabra aside as a sanctuary for its unique wildlife.

As many as 150,000 of the tortoises may still survive on Aldabra today, judging from current population studies. Zoologists consider them the oldest of all terrestrial vertebrates. A German expedition to the Seychelle Islands, several hundred miles north of Aldabra, viewed a specimen in 1899 that was said to have been brought from Aldabra a century before. On Saint Helena one tortoise that was said to have been there when the exiled Napoleon arrived in 1815 still survived in 1967.

Aldabra is administered by Great Britain, and in the 1960s the British Government readied plans to build an airfield and military staging area on the atoll. There was immediate protest from wildlife conservationists, for such development spelled certain doom to the tortoises as well as to various birds that lived and nested there. Aldabra is the home of a rare, flightless rail and is also the principal breeding grounds for the pink-footed booby and most of the frigate birds of the Indian Ocean.

Due to the protests—and perhaps also because it could ill afford the money needed for the development—Britain abandoned the plans for the airfield. For the moment the tortoises remain safe. The only long-term action that will guarantee their survival, however, is to set the whole atoll aside as a permanent and inviolable wildlife sanctuary.

A Heavy Toll of Vanishing Species

Dodos and giant tortoises and the Mauritius kestrel are not the only species that have disappeared from the islands of the Indian Ocean. The full toll since these islands were settled is staggering. Animals living on small oceanic islands are particularly vulnerable to the changes brought about by man, and the species native to Indian Ocean islands have been especially victimized. The Mascarenes have what is probably the world's worst record for extinction, with the Hawaiian Islands their only rival.

According to the best current estimates, about 90 percent of the birds native to the Mascarenes have become extinct since their settlement. The sorry summary follows: eight birds extinct on Réunion, eleven on Mauritius, eleven on Rodriguez. Included among them are the dodos and solitaire, as well as a flightless blue rail, a flightless night heron, three parakeets, a parrot, three owls, and two kinds of starling. Several lizards have also been exterminated.

But that is not all. Those species that still survive are threatened with the same ultimate fate because of the inroads man has made—and is continuing to make—on the islands. The small island of Réunion has a present population of nearly half a million people, more than 500 per square mile. The population density on Mauritius is much greater, 850,000 packed into 720 square miles or about 1200 people per square mile. Little wonder that most of the island has been stripped of its forest cover. As for Rodriguez, practically none of its native vegetation is left. Almost any wildlife species would find survival in such an inhospitable area difficult.

The losses on the Seychelles have not been quite so bad. Only one bird, the Seychelles white-eye, is extinct. Eight other species are threatened, including the Seychelles kestrel, a parrot, an owl, and the magpie robin.

Madagascar's extinction record for wildlife is tragically similar to that of the Mascarenes. All in all, some thirty mammals, eleven birds, and at least one reptile are classified as endangered species. Each is disappearing because of man's activities. Some 70 percent of the natural vegetation has already been destroyed according to current estimates. And every year some forty or fifty additional square miles of habitat are destroyed to make room for growing rice, bananas, and vegetables. The island population, now at eight million people, increases at a rate of 3 percent yearly.

A man's wealth in Madagascar has traditionally been valued in cattle. Today ten million African Zebu cattle roam the grasslands, overgrazing them and turning them into near desert in some areas, especially in the south. The custom of burning off the grass every year to clear the land for cultivation has also hastened the destruction of the land.

Little wonder that Madagascar's unique flora and fauna are in deadly peril today. Some sanctuaries and nature preserves have been set aside, as already noted, but many more are needed if some of the earth's most fascinating creatures are to have any chance for survival.

Situated upon the Equator, and bathed by the tepid water of the great tropical oceans, this region enjoys a climate more uniformly hot and moist than almost any other part of the globe, and teems with natural productions, which are elsewhere unknown. The richest of fruits and the most precious of spices are here indigenous.   Alfred Russell Wallace

6

THE MALAY ARCHIPELAGO

Lying between the continental land masses of Asia to the north and Australia to the south is a watery world of warm seas spotted with some ten thousand islands or more that make up the Malay Archipelago. Clustered around the equator, these steamy tropical lands show infinite variety: coastal mangrove swamps and lush jungles; coral atolls and soaring mountain ranges; fiery volcanoes and lofty summits capped with snow; grassy plateaus and sandy, palm-fringed beaches. Flanked by the two great land masses, the myriad islands form a series of stepping-stones over which animals and plants from both continents have traveled. The islands in the center provide a meeting place for both Asiatic and Australian forms.

The northernmost group are the Philippines—more than

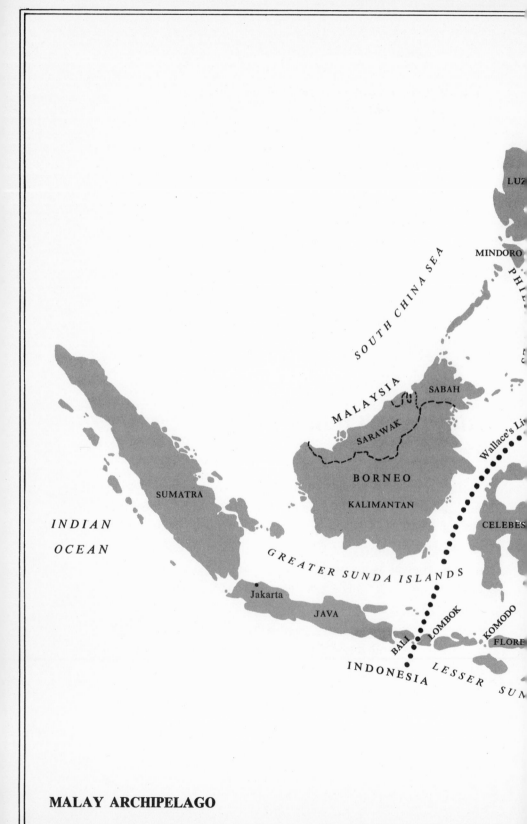

MALAY ARCHIPELAGO

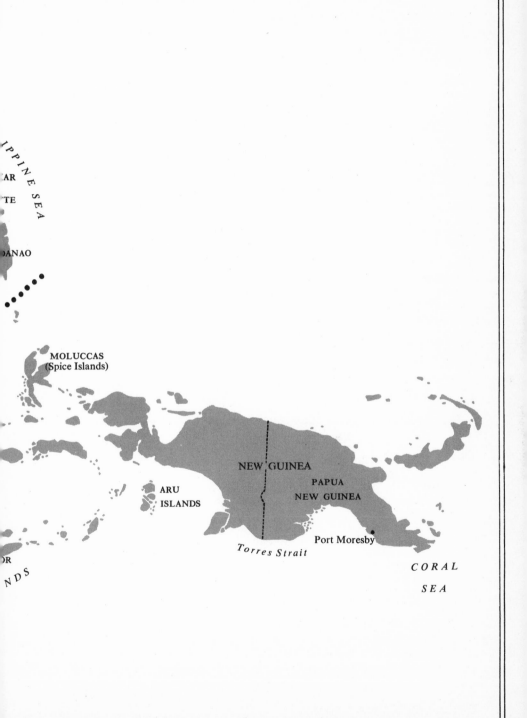

PHILIPPINE SEA

AR

TE

ANAO

MOLUCCAS
(Spice Islands)

NEW GUINEA

PAPUA
NEW GUINEA

ARU
ISLANDS

Port Moresby

Torres Strait

OR

NDS

CORAL

SEA

seven thousand islands, the vast majority of them tiny, uninhabited, and unnamed. Ninety-five percent of the land is included in eleven main islands, the two largest being Luzon in
the north and Mindanao in the south.

South and east of the Philippines lies the vast and still partially unexplored island of New Guinea, a mysterious land
fringed by dense equatorial jungles and impenetrable coastal
swamps, with a backbone of mountains soaring as high as 16,000
feet. After Greenland, it is the world's second largest island,
stretching 1500 miles from east to west through the western
Pacific.

Reaching in a great 3000-mile arc westward from New
Guinea lie the East Indies—some 1300 islands in all. Farthest
toward the setting sun is Sumatra, which flanks the coast of the
Malayan Peninsula like a huge finger pointing across the Bay
of Bengal toward India.

Sumatra, Java, Celebes, and Borneo make up the Greater
Sunda Islands, one of the two major island groups of the East
Indies. The other group, the Lesser Sundas, consists of a number
of much smaller islands—Bali, Lombok, Timor, and many
others—that stretch eastward from Java. A smaller but important group of islands lies between New Guinea and Celebes—
the Moluccas, or Spice Islands. The treasured spices grown on
these islands were what brought about much of the early trade
between the East and West, which stimulated the search for a
new route to the Indies, which launched the great voyages of
exploration undertaken by Vasco da Gama, Christopher Columbus, and Ferdinand Magellan.

Once part of the continent of Asia, the East Indies were
separated from the mainland during the Pleistocene, when the
great ice caps and glaciers melted and the levels of the seas rose.
New Guinea, which had been linked to Australia, was separated
from that southern continent in the same way.

A Mix of People

The native peoples of the Malay Archipelago are a be-guiling and bewildering mix, the result of different races that successively migrated from Asia during and after the Pleistocene. The first to come were the most primitive groups. They were pushed out by more advanced peoples and forced either to move on to other islands or to retreat deep into the jungles or high onto the slopes of rugged mountains. Most of the natives of New Guinea are dark-skinned Melanesians. Many of them until several generations ago were primitive hunters. Primitive Pygmy Negritos still live high in the mountains of the island's interior.

The earliest inhabitants of the Philippines were also Negritos. They were followed by Malayans and other more advanced groups from Asia. But as recently as 1970 a small group called the Tasaday were discovered deep in the rain forests of Min-danao, living a Stone Age existence. Fewer than one hundred in number, the Tasaday are food gatherers and hunters, with no knowledge of agriculture or working with metals. As with other endangered groups, the Tasaday will probably disappear as a result of their discovery and exploitation by modern techno-logical man.

As succeeding groups of human beings populated the East Indies, a complex mixture gradually resulted. Melanesians mixed with Malayans, and yellow, brown, and white races added their genes to the pool. Hindus from India invaded Java and Sumatra sometime during the past two thousand years, and Moslems con-quered Java in the fifteenth century. The Arabs, of course, had been trading with India and the Far East for many centuries before that time.

The Lure of the Spice Islands

Before the sixteenth century, however, this whole vast region of some ten thousand islands—the Malay Archipelago—was practically unknown to Europeans. Marco Polo touched at Java and Sumatra in the year 1292, when he was on his way home after serving the Great Khan, and told a little about life on these islands in his writings. Various products of the East Indies were also known in Europe at that time—especially the highly prized spices that reached the continent over ancient caravan routes or through trade with the Arabs.

All of the spices—but especially clove, cinnamon, nutmeg, mace, and pepper—were treasured articles of commerce. "They were part of life in both the European and Asiatic worlds," historian Samuel Elliot Morrison observes. "They flavored all kinds of cooked food. They were used in perfumes and (like myrrh) for embalming. Spices were among the most important ingredients of *materia medica.*"

Spices stimulated many voyages of exploration during the late fifteenth and early sixteenth centuries in traders' efforts to find new and easier routes to the Indies. The idea of a western route across the Atlantic from Europe to the Spice Islands prompted the Spanish monarchs, Isabella and Ferdinand, to back Christopher Columbus in his epochal voyages of exploration.

New Routes to the Indies

On his first voyage in 1492, and on subsequent voyages as well, Columbus found that a western route to the East Indies posed many difficulties. His main idea was correct, but instead of the Spice Islands he discovered a New World—North and South America—that blocked his way to the Pacific and the East Indies.

Heading southward from Portugal in 1497, the mariner Vasco da Gama successfully demonstrated that sailing to the Indies by an eastern route was possible. He was the first European to take his ships around Africa's southern tip and eastward across the Indian Ocean to Calicut on the Malabar Coast of India. From that point the sail is a short one, comparatively speaking, to the East Indies. Following him in quick succession, many other European navigators reached the East Indies by traveling the same route.

Columbus had been blocked by the New World in the west, but Ferdinand Magellan, sailing for Spain a generation later, finally did find the western route to the Indies. Leaving Europe in 1519, he sailed across the Atlantic, then southward along the eastern coast of South America. Eventually he reached the continent's tip, sailed westward through the straits that are named for him, and onward through the great South Sea, which was so calm and benign that he named it Pacific.

Reaching Mactan in the Philippine Islands in March, 1519, Magellan found not savages but people with an advanced culture and social system. Wishing to gain favor with the local sultan, he made the mistake of getting mixed up in local politics and backing his host in warfare with a neighboring ruler. Magellan paid for that mistake with his life on April 27, killed in battle off Mactan.

His companions sailed on to Borneo and then to the Spice Islands, where they were ceremoniously welcomed by the Sultan of Tidore, who gave them two bird-of-paradise skins to take back as gifts to the Spanish monarchs.

Portuguese mariners had visited the Spice Islands a few years earlier, however. They soon returned and subdued the garrison that the Spaniards had left behind. From that time on the East Indies became pawns in a colonial power struggle among many European nations: Spain and Portugal at first, the Dutch and English soon thereafter, and finally the French and Germans.

By 1601 the Dutch were firmly entrenched at the Cape of

Good Hope. From this strategic vantage point they controlled the eastern route to the Indies and as a result had already mounted at least fifteen expeditions to the East Indies. The Dutch East India Company was formed, and soon the Netherlands claimed most of the East Indies as their colonial empire. The Portuguese kept a toehold in the Far East at Timor. The British and then the Germans staked out protectorates in New Guinea. Spain, driven from the Indies by the Dutch, took over the Philippine Islands until 1898 when they were ousted by the United States.

Wallace's Line

Alfred Russell Wallace, a British naturalist, traveled and collected zoological specimens in New Guinea and the East Indies from 1854 to 1862. In 1869, he described his experiences in a classic book of natural history, *The Malay Archipelago*. A careful observer and thinker, Wallace visited many islands of the East Indies and was struck by the fact that neighboring islands often supported very different kinds of plants and animals.

On the islands west of a certain imaginary line he noted that the fauna was largely Asian in origin. East of that line the Australian influence was dominant. After long thought and observation, Wallace established the line of demarcation— known ever since as Wallace's Line—between what he said were the Indo-Malaysian and the Austro-Malaysian zoogeographical regions.

Today zoogeographers recognize that line as separating two great faunal areas—the Oriental and the Australian. Going from north to south (as shown on the map, pages 186-187), Wallace's Line passes below the Philippines, then turns southward between Celebes and Borneo, and through the narrow passage between Bali and Lombok. These last two tiny islands are just a few miles apart, but each supports a very different and distinct fauna. All of the islands to the north and west of Wallace's Line have predominantly Asiatic animals. All to the south and east have animals that are typically Australian. There are some islands close to either side of the line that support a mixture of the two.

New Nations

Since World War II the islands of the Malay Archipelago have been largely freed from colonialism and now pursue their destinies as independent nations. The Philippines were granted their freedom by the United States in 1946. The states of Sarawak and Sabah in northern Borneo are today part of the independent nation of Malaysia, while Kalimantan, the larger southern portion of the island, is now a part of the Republic of Indonesia.

Indonesia, a teeming country of 3000 islands and 125 million people, includes all of the old Dutch East Indies as well as the western half of New Guinea, which is now known as Irian Jaya, or West Irian. The eastern half of the island, known as Papua New Guinea, is one of the newest of all independent nations. Made up of former German, British, and Australian colonies and protectorates, it was granted its independence in 1975. Many of its population of 2.5 million people are still struggling to emerge from a primitive way of life.

For each of these new nations, the problems of feeding the population and the strenuous efforts being launched to advance the country's economy have taken up most of the people's efforts. Little time is spent on conservation, but old preserves are still guarded and many other areas of natural habitat are largely untouched. With each passing year, however, the situation is changing—often for the worse.

Javan rhinoceros

JAVAN AND SUMATRAN RHINOCEROSES

Rhinoceros sondaicus and *Didermocerus sumatrensis*

Stopping at the islands of Java and Sumatra in the year 1292, Marco Polo noted that in the kingdom of Pasei: "There are wild elephants in the country, and numerous unicorns, which are very nearly as big. They have hair like that of a buffalo, feet like those of an elephant, and a horn in the middle of the forehead, which is black and very thick. . . ."

These "unicorns" of which he spoke were none other than one-horned Javan rhinoceroses. Somewhat smaller than the great Indian rhinoceros, this species has armor-plated skin that is similarly folded but without the round rivet marks of its larger relative. It once was found on the Asian mainland from Burma to Malaya and ranged through Java, Sumatra, and Borneo as well. Until a century ago it was quite abundant in many of these areas. Like the Indian rhinoceros, however, it was hunted mercilessly. Colonial sportsmen often hunted the Javan rhinoceros merely for fun during the nineteenth and early twentieth centuries, and poachers would go to almost any lengths to kill it for its valuable horn and other parts.

As the inevitable result, the Javan rhino had disappeared almost everywhere by 1900. An estimated fifty of them survived in Java, and perhaps a dozen or so remained in Sumatra. There may even have been a few hunted stragglers on the mainland, but they were soon exterminated. The Sumatran remnant vanished as well, and Java seemed to be the only area where the Javan rhinoceros was found.

In a determined effort to protect the species, Dutch officials in Java established the 117-square mile Udjung Kulon Nature Reserve in 1921 on the western tip of the island. Later made a game reserve, this wild area helped to protect other threatened species such as the Javan tiger, the wild ox or banteng, the rusa deer, the chevrotain, various gibbons and hornbills, and the green peafowl, as well as the Javan rhinoceros.

At this time, no more than twenty Javan rhinos were thought to survive. Slowly they increased to thirty or more at the start of World War II in 1939. After the war, the new nation of Indonesia continued to protect the reserve in spite of many difficulties, and by 1960 the rhinoceros population was thought to be about thirty-five in Java's Udjung Kulon Reserve. Poachers invaded the sanctuary in 1963 and 1964, however, and killed at least seven. Since then, as a result of rigid protection, the population has increased to about fifty.

It is now believed that a few specimens, perhaps as many as twenty, have also survived in Sumatra's Leuser Reserve. Even with these increases, the Javan rhinoceros is probably the world's rarest big-game animal today.

Another Asiatic rhinoceros is the Sumatran two-horned species. Smallest of the rhinos, it once ranged throughout southeastern Asia, as well as through Sumatra, Java, and Borneo. Its hide is not pleated like that of its two relatives, but is covered with considerably more hair. There are two recognized races; the mainland form is sometimes known as the hairy-eared rhinoceros. Both it and the island form have followed the same trail to oblivion as their relatives.

Once abundant in the Mekong Delta of southern Indochina, common throughout most of its range in the early years of the twentieth century, the Sumatran rhinoceros has in the years since been killed off nearly everywhere. Today the entire population numbers probably no more than two or three hundred animals. Some forty to eighty of them are concentrated in and around the Leuser Reserve in northern Sumatra. Burma, as recorded by the IUCN in 1973, may have two dozen survivors. Thailand has perhaps ten to twenty, and Malaya about the same number. These figures may err on the side of optimism, however, for the hunting and poaching go on relentlessly.

ORANGUTAN
Pongo pygmaeus

A troop of gibbons swing through the treetops likes circus acrobats, their whoops echoing far and wide through the Bornean forest. A big, helmeted hornbill flies past them, heading for the tree where his mate incubates eggs in a nest cavity. A huge red ape appears, carefully walking along a high branch with arms outspread like a tightrope walker. And squatting on the limb, the orangutan seizes a nearby cluster of fruit and begins to eat.

One of the four kinds of great ape—the others are the gorilla, chimpanzee, and the gibbon—the orangutan ranged widely throughout suitable forest habitat in southeastern Asia during the Pleistocene era. Within historic times, however, it has been limited to the islands of Borneo and Sumatra and was first made known to Western science in the mid-seventeenth century by William Bontius, a Dutch doctor in Borneo. The first detailed description of the species in its natural habitat was written little

more than a century ago by the English naturalist, Alfred Russell Wallace.

On one occasion in Borneo, after killing an adult female orang, Wallace found a helpless infant nearby and attempted to raise it, remarking on what an affectionate and trusting baby it was. He did not have milk or other proper food for the infant, however, and it died after three months, much to his sorrow.

An adult male orangutan may weigh nearly two hundred pounds while the female commonly weighs half that amount. Zoo specimens often weigh a great deal more, for they are more sedentary. A big male seldom stands taller than four feet, two inches, but his long arms spread from side to side may span nearly eight feet. The coat of both sexes ranges from a warm red color to dark brown. Most mature males develop wide, leathery cheek pads, as well as a throat or laryngeal sac, and an old male may grow a beard. The expression "orangutan" means "man of the woods" in Malayan, a very suitable name for this great ape.

In the wild, orangutans inhabit lowland rain forests and swampy wooded areas. Their chief food is fruit, such as figs and pulpy durian. They live a nomadic existence, wandering through the forest in family groups or as solitary individuals. At nightfall, all except the largest and heaviest males make sleeping nests for themselves in the trees, drawing limbs together within a fork and fashioning a mattress of leaves and branches. During wet weather they sometimes construct a sheltering roof over the nest.

During World War II the homeland of the orangutan suffered severe upheavals as both Borneo and Sumatra were captured by the Japanese, then retaken by Allied armies. Even more unrest followed when the Indonesians forced the Dutch colonials out of Sumatra and southern Borneo (Kalimantan). For a number of years afterward there was sporadic fighting between the forces of Indonesia and Malaysia—both newly independent countries—for control of Sarawak and Sabah in northern Borneo. In addition, much natural habitat was destroyed through deforestation, and many orangs were killed or captured for sale to zoos, so not surprisingly the population of this great ape has dwindled steadily during the past thirty years. Today its numbers are estimated at perhaps 5000. About 2000 live in Sabah, 700 in Sarawak, and 1000 in Kalimantan; the rest, perhaps 1000, inhabit northern Sumatra, most of them in the area around the Leuser Reserve.

Today the orangutan is protected in both Borneo and Sumatra, but illegal hunting and the smuggling of live specimens still go on. A young orang may sell for $5000 or more, and for that kind of money many poachers are willing to take plenty of risks. The usual methods involve the shooting of an adult female with a baby, and then capturing the youngster. Captive young are smuggled out to Singapore or Hong Kong, where they are supplied with forged papers and certificates so that they may be sold abroad. For every young orang that ends up alive and well in captivity, an estimated seven or eight others die. Some are shot during capture; others die in captivity because of injuries, disease, or improper care.

In 1962, the American Association of Zoological Parks and Aquariums established a boycott on illegal trade in orangutans and several other endangered species, including gorillas and monkey-eating eagles. At that time all illegally captured orangutans that were confiscated by Malaysian Government officials were turned over to reputable zoos for raising, since captured babies had little chance to survive if released directly back into the wild.

In Sarawak, however, Mrs. Barbara Harrisson, wife of the director of the Sarawak Museum, started a rehabilitation center, where young orangs seized from poachers could be cared for and prepared for eventual release into their native habitat. A similar program was later instituted by the Forest Department in Sabah, which set up an orangutan rehabilitation center in the Sepilok Forest Reserve.

At the initiative of Mrs. Harrisson, the hunting and trading of orangs in Indonesian Borneo and in Sumatra were sharply reduced in 1968 when an agreement was negotiated between Indonesia's conservation authorities and the Survival Service Commission of the IUCN. Under the provisions of this agreement no orangs could be exported from Indonesia without SSC clearance and papers. In 1969, the world's bona fide zoos willingly agreed to this restriction. In the years since, the Indonesian Forestry Service has established one rehabilitation center for confiscated orangs in the Tanjung Puting Reserve in Kalimantan as well as two similar centers in northern Sumatra. One, the Langhat Reserve, is supported by the Frankfurt Zoological Society in Germany.

In 1974, there was a worldwide total of 625 captive orangutans in 131 zoos and other institutions. Of these animals, 226 were born in captivity. A record book of all captive orangs and their breeding success is kept at the Yerkes Regional Primate Research Center at Emory University in Atlanta, Georgia.

TAMARAU AND ANOA
Bubalus (Anoa) mindorensis and *B.(A.) depressicornis*

Just to the south of the main Philippine island of Luzon lies the island of Mindoro. About eighty miles long by fifty wide, it is lapped on the west by the South China Sea, and to the south by the Sulu Sea. Along its backbone is a range of rugged mountains, some towering nearly 8000 feet high. The wild interior is the home of a tribal group known as the Mangyanes. It is also the last refuge of the tamarau, one of the smallest and most endangered of all wild cattle.

Standing about three feet, nine inches at the shoulder, the tamarau is mostly dark gray, with a white crescent on the throat. Its short horns sweep backward from the face and are creased with many transverse grooves. Wild and elusive, the tamarau inhabits forested areas and thick stands of cane and bamboo.

When the species was first described scientifically in 1889, there was a flourishing population of perhaps ten thousand animals on Mindoro. Its numbers, however, steadily dropped during the next half century as the island became increasingly cleared and cultivated and as settlers poured in from other islands. The Japanese occupied Mindoro during World War II. Afterward, there were no more than an estimated one thousand tamarau left, and their future did not seem very promising.

When the war ended, new settlers poured into Mindoro. Swamps were drained, forests cleared, and a successful malarial control program was launched, allowing even more land to be opened up for agriculture. Firearms were prevalent after the wartime years, and hunting the little wild cattle was a popular pastime. Mindoro is only ten hours by car and boat from Manila, and many hunters from the big city took advantage of this proximity to bag a tamarau or two. By 1953 only 250 or so survived in mountain areas. Eleven years later, when conservationist Lee Talbot and his wife visited the island, they found only scattered pockets of tamarau surviving in three small areas.

One of these was the Mount Calavite area in northern Mindoro. This region had been proclaimed a preserve in 1920, but had been given little actual protection. In fact, more tamarau were probably killed there than almost anywhere else.

Another area around Mount Iglit in the southeastern part of the island was declared a game reserve in 1960. Ranching was allowed in the reserve, however, and ranchers and their friends often indulged in shooting sprees against the little wild cattle, which from their point of view were nuisances to proper ranching because they competed with domestic livestock for food. In 1968, at least seventeen tamarau were reported killed in one such hunt in this area.

Backed by the World Wildlife Fund and the Survival Service Commission of the IUCN, Dr. Tom Harrisson surveyed Mindoro in 1969 and concluded that no more than 100 tamarau were left. Through his efforts, and those of Charles A. Lindbergh, who promoted wildlife conservation around the world, the Philippine Wildlife Conservation Association was formed. Hunting of the tamarau was formally outlawed, and protection of the sanctuaries was strengthened. The Mount Iglit area was increased in size, and a research team sent to study animals there. A third sanctuary, Mount Mitchell, was established in the Sablayon area. In 1971, about 148 animals were counted on the island.

A thousand miles to the south of Mindoro lies Celebes, one of the Greater Sunda Islands. It is the home of the lowland anoa *Bubalus (Anoa) depressicornis,* smallest of all wild cattle. Standing a little over three feet at the shoulder, this species is dark

anoa

brown or black, with white markings on the throat and lower jaw. It is endangered for the same reasons that its relative the tamarau is—loss of habitat, hunting, and too little legal protection. In the mountainous highlands of the island lives a somewhat different form, the mountain anoa, which some zoologists consider a distinct species—*Bubalus (Anoa) quarlesi*. The mountain anoa is also approaching extinction.

In 1970, there were eighteen specimens of the lowland anoa in nine zoos. Some of these zoos have had success in breeding the species in captivity, and the IUCN has established a stud book to record the captive births.

PHILIPPINE MONKEY-EATING EAGLE
Pithecophaga jefferyi

Exploring the Philippine island of Samar in 1896, the English naturalist John Whitehead collected an eagle then unknown to science. In his notes, Whitehead remarked: "He is well known to the natives as a robber of their poultry and small pigs, but chiefly as a destroyer of monkeys which are the only animals sufficiently abundant to support such a large bird."

One of the most magnificent of all the world's feathered species, the monkey-eating eagle has a wingspread of eight feet or more. Its sleek plumage is a combination of dark brown and cinnamon with some black markings, with underparts that are mostly white. It has fierce gray eyes, a shaggy crest, and a huge, sharply hooked beak. Its former range included the islands of Mindanao, Luzon, Samar, and Leyte. It nests in huge kapok and mahogany trees, high on the forested mountain slopes, and raises only one young each year. The prey of the species includes squirrels, monkeys, and colugos, or "flying lemurs," unique gliding mammals that are placed in an order of their own, the Dermoptera, or "skin wings."

Never plentiful, the monkey-eating eagle has long been a prized trophy for hunters, as well as a valuable addition to any zoo collection. Natives of the Philippines once killed it as a menace to their poultry. Forestry operations and agricultural clearing that destroyed much of its needed habitat have also contributed to the eagle's decline. In 1969, for example, the

Philippine Free Press reported that deforestation in Mindanao was occurring at the incredible rate of two and a half acres every three minutes. Whether those figures are reliable or not, they do illustrate the vast changes that are taking place on the island. In 1976, the human population of the Philippines was more than forty-one million people, and it is growing at the rate of nearly 3 percent each year.

As a result of all these adverse factors, the monkey-eating eagle is one of the world's rarest birds, with probably no more than forty or fifty remaining in the wild. Most of them inhabit the area in or around Mount Apo National Park on Mindanao.

Recognizing the danger of its imminent extinction, the American Association of Zoological Parks and Aquariums established a boycott of illegal trade in the species in 1962. In 1967, the same organization passed a resolution prohibiting any of its members from selling, trading, capturing, or accepting a monkey-eating eagle as a gift, with the exception of those made available by governments or conservation organizations.

In 1969, Charles Lindbergh donated a captive monkey-eating eagle that he had secured to the Philippine Parks and Wildlife Commission, to launch a campaign aimed at returning all captive birds to the wild. This campaign, however, has not been successful. The Philippine Government has extended legal protection to the species today, but additional reserves are needed for it in the wild.

The monkey-eating eagle has never been bred successfully in captivity. Several experimental programs have been initiated, however, including the attempted pairing of a female at the Los Angeles Zoo with a male specimen lent by the New York Zoological Society. This much-traveled male bird had been sent to the Philadelphia Zoo several years before on a similar mission with that zoo's female. Both attempts failed. With time and new experimental techniques, however, it is hoped that this beautiful species may eventually reproduce in captivity, for the future of the monkey-eating eagle may well hinge on its captive breeding success.

KOMODO MONITOR
Varanus komodensis

Off the western tip of Flores, one of the Lesser Sunda Islands, lie three tiny islands—Rintja, Padar, and Komodo. Komodo, the largest of the three, is about twenty-five miles long by twelve miles wide. These islands are the home of the giant lizard known as the Komodo monitor, or Komodo dragon.

In 1912, a pioneering Dutch aviator from Java made a forced landing on Komodo, an island that was then practically unknown even to the Dutch who ruled over it by colonial claim. There, much to his astonishment, the airman saw what looked like huge dragons, some of them measuring ten feet or more in length. He carried tales of these fearsome creatures back to Java with him and, after further investigation, the director of the zoological museum in Buitenzorg (now Bogor, south of Dja-karta, in western Java), published a description of this Komodo dragon.

Male Komodo monitors may measure ten feet in length and weigh more than two hundred pounds. Some early observers re-ported specimens nearly thirteen feet in length and correspond-ingly heavier. Females are smaller than the males, seldom measuring more than eight feet. The adults have a tough beaded skin that varies from a dull grayish brown to black. Many platelets embedded in the skin make it almost useless in the hide trade. Chinese hunters killed the monitor in the old days, nevertheless, and sold "dragon's-tail oil" as a remedy for burns and other ailments.

The adult monitors are too heavy to climb trees, but the young are active climbers. They are much more brightly marked

than the adults, with orange throat and belly and golden spots dotting the gray-black back. Whatever its age, every Komodo monitor is equipped with a long forked tongue, which it uses as a sense organ for touching and smelling food. Adults are mainly scavengers and eat such carrion as the carcasses of deer, goats, pigs, and other smaller animals. On occasion they also stalk and kill live prey. They are voracious eaters, and one recent investigator who spent a year studying the species on Komodo reported that a female monitor eight and a half feet long and weighing about one hundred pounds ate all of a ninety-pound pig at one time.

From December through March of each year the "islands of the thousand dragons" have monsoon rains. They are quite dry during the rest of the year, and the monitors retreat into burrows to protect themselves from the hot sun and high temperatures.

The Indonesian Government has declared Rintja, Padar, and Komodo as reserves for the species, and approximately two thousand monitors survive on the three islands today. Since 1956, the Government has allowed an average of only four Komodo monitors to be collected annually for scientific studies or exhibition. As of 1974 there were nineteen specimens in nine different zoos. Five of them were bred in captivity at the Surabaja Zoo in Java.

BIRDS OF PARADISE
Family Paradisaeidae

Visiting the Molucca Islands shortly after Magellan's death, the surviving members of his expedition were presented with several bird-of-paradise skins that had been prepared and dried in the customary Malay manner, with legs and wings removed. The Malays called the birds "manuk dewata," or God's birds.

Returning to Spain in 1522, the pioneering circumnavigators of the world presented the skins to their sovereign, the king of Spain. Antonio Pigafetta, the chronicler of the voyage, duly mentioned the gift to the king and recorded: "These birds have no wings but instead of them, long feathers of different colors like plumes. They never fly except when the wind blows." Birds of the Sun is what the Spaniards called these wondrous creatures that had no legs but bore lustrous plumes. "Their true home," wrote one inspired naturalist, "is the terrestrial Paradise where their sole sustenance is the dew of heaven."

Drawing upon such misleading and inaccurate reports, Edward Topsell in the early 1600s declared: "It is a Maxime with Aristotle that there are no birdes without feete. . . . But it appeareth most playnelie that Aristotle was deceaved in this, because hee never sawe a bird of Paradise." But even in Topsell's time, no European had as yet seen a living bird of paradise.

In 1820, Temminck, a wealthy Dutchman, sent an expedition to the East Indies to search for birds of paradise. Not only did the expedition experience no luck in its quest, but, even worse, most of the members of the expedition fell victim to either fever or the arrows of unfriendly natives. The French scientist, René Lesson, was the first European of record to see living specimens when he observed two species of birds of paradise in New Guinea in 1824.

The first white man to study birds of paradise in the wild, collect numerous specimens, and write of their true nature was Alfred Russell Wallace. All in all, he collected specimens of five different species of birds of paradise and added a great deal to the knowledge of the family.

greater bird of paradise

Collecting in the Aru Islands, home of the greater bird of paradise, he graphically depicted the courtship dance of these beautiful birds. The males in breeding plumage are resplendant in rich chestnut, gold, and emerald-green plumage, and they bear shimmering two-foot-long plumes of lemon yellow on each flank. Wallace recorded that during the month of May the birds would start their " 'sacaleli,' or dancing parties in certain trees in the forest . . . which have an immense head of spreading branches and large but scattered leaves, giving a clear space for the birds to play and exhibit their plumes." A dozen or more birds would assemble at these trees, he noted, raising and vibrating their plumes for the benefit of the drab and inconspicuous females. Native Papuans prized the beauty of the plumes for ceremonial wear and shot the birds with arrows tipped with conical wooden caps that would stun or kill the victim without piercing the skin or injuring the plumage in any way. To do so, each hunter would build an inconspicuous platform blind high in the treetops, covering it with a leafy roof under which he could hide. They would climb into this shelter before daybreak and wait there for the birds to assemble and start their dance.

As we know today, different species of birds of paradise bear courtship plumes on different parts of the body: some on the flanks, others on the head, the wings, the throat, the back, or the rump. Many of their feathers are iridescent like those of the hummingbird.

The five species that Wallace was able to collect were all lowland or island forms. There were many other kinds in the New Guinea highlands, as Wallace knew, but in spite of every effort, he was unable to get any. Even then bird-of-paradise plumes were valuable articles of commerce to the chiefs of the coastal villages. They obtained the skins at a low rate from mountain tribesmen and sold them to traders at a high profit. In addition, they used many plumes for their own ceremonials, or "sing-sings." As a consequence, these coastal chiefs did not want any meddling Europeans to spoil their lucrative trade. Therefore, they would not help Wallace collect in the highlands.

Returning to England in 1862, Wallace brought with him two healthy male specimens of the lesser bird of paradise, which thrived at the London Zoo for one and two years respectively. The first live birds of paradise seen in the Western World, they aroused great admiration and undoubtedly stimulated the sale of bird-of-paradise plumes and skins, which were greatly prized for the millinery trade.

In the late years of the nineteenth century the traffic in plumes grew to enormous volume, with fifty to one hundred thousand skins sold annually in the major headquarters of the feather trade in Paris, Amsterdam, London, New York, and other centers. William T. Hornaday, in *Our Vanishing Wildlife,* quotes the prices for skins in London in 1911 as follows: $10.32 to $21.00 for each greater bird-of-paradise skin; $1.44 to $1.80 for the twelve-wired; $2.50 and $2.40 respectively for the red and king birds of paradise. Hornaday also noted that Argus pheasant skins from Asia sold at $3.60 each, golden pheasants at 34¢ to 46¢, and hummingbird skins from South America were worth just 2¢ apiece. The voracious feather trade was devastating to many species of birds all over the world.

Luckily for the birds of paradise and many others, the United States banned the import of such plumes in 1913, and Mexico swiftly followed suit. Birds of paradise had been depleted by years of killing, and only 30,000 skins were brought into London for sale that year. The trade dwindled even more, and England finally banned the import of plumes in 1921. At last the deadly plumage trade was stopped on a worldwide basis, and just in time. Native New Guineans continued to take the birds, but mainly for use in their ceremonials.

Today ornithologists recognize some forty-four different kinds of birds of paradise—even more if the closely related rifle birds and manucodes are included. Perhaps the last bird of paradise to be discovered was the ribbon-tailed species, which was found by ornithologist Fred Shaw-Meyer in 1938. The survival of all of these beautiful and interesting birds depends upon strict regulations covering the capture of living birds and the export of plumes.

Years ago Australia barred all hunting of birds of paradise

in its eastern half of New Guinea (Papua), except for those taken by local people hunting with bows in order to get plumes for their annual sing-sings. These traditional celebrations have proven to be lucrative tourist attractions, and as many as twenty thousand Papuans take part each year. Each of the performers, as calculated by conservationist Kai Curry-Lindahl, is adorned on the average with five bird-of-paradise skins. If correct, the total adds up to about one hundred thousand bird-of-paradise plumes used for each sing-sing. The plumes are traded as items of wealth, as observed by Christopher Healey, a conservation researcher in the field for the New York Zoological Society. He reported in 1974: ". . . rights to hunt various sections of forest for birds of paradise are fixed in the traditions of various cultures and villages." In 1965, the Australian New Guinea House of Assembly introduced a bill to legalize the killing of birds of paradise, evidently in order to stimulate the native economy and tourist trade. Luckily the bill was voted down.

Still, many people are as eager as ever to acquire plumes, and several species are severely threatened by overhunting. In 1969, it was reported that at least four species—the ribbon-tailed, the Princess Stephanie, the blue, and the King of Saxony birds of paradise—were menaced by overhunting and the "massive export" of plumes to mountain tribes for ceremonial regalia. Some highland species have been largely shot out of existence in many areas. As a consequence, mountain tribes must get their plumes elsewhere, and in the process laws are generally flouted.

Other Animals of the East Indies

In 1945, zoologist Francis Harper listed eleven species of animals that were vanishing in the Malay Archipelago, among them the orangutan, the Sumatran elephant, the Javan and Sumatran rhinos, the babirussa, or wild pig, and the various species of wild oxen—anoas, bantengs, and the serow. All of these ani-

Malay tapir

mals are still threatened today, but none has vanished completely.

The Javan tiger—very rare by 1936—may now be extinct, and the Bali tiger is feared gone as well. In Sumatra, the beautiful golden cat is now rare and may soon disappear entirely on the islands. The same can be said of the black-and-white Malayan tapir, the proboscis monkey of Borneo, and the beautiful Javan, or green, peafowl.

New Guinea echidna

In New Guinea, the dominant mammalian species are tree kangaroos, cuscuses, and the peculiar long-beaked echidna. All of them—and many smaller species as well—are hunted by the people for food. The introduction of modern shotguns, and the destruction of forest habitat contributes to the dwindling fortunes of many of these mammals and to those of the cassowary, a huge flightless bird, as well. The New Guinea harpy eagle, closest living relative of the Philippine monkey-eating eagle, is being taken as a hunting trophy, and the two species of New Guinea crocodiles are prized for their skins. And just as the birds of paradise are hunted for their colorful plumes, the great birdwing butterflies, found only in New Guinea and neighboring islands, are eagerly hunted as collectors' items. In 1967, one rare specimen is said to have sold for $2500.

Arguing the case for national parks and reserves in Papua, New Guinea, several years ago, one concerned scientist observed: "An effective *preventative* conservation programme is the need of the moment."

The Australian continent has been described as a colossal natural-history museum stocked with living fossils.   Ellis Troughton

7

AUSTRALIA, STRANGE LAND DOWN UNDER

Although European geographers of the Middle Ages and before had no reliable reports to back them up, they spoke of a great unknown southern continent—*Terra Australis Incognito,* the Unknown Southland—that they concluded must exist somewhere in the southern hemisphere as a counterbalance to the great land masses of the northern hemisphere. Long before the Middle Ages, however, the ancient Chinese and other highly civilized peoples of southeastern Asia and the Malay Archipelago knew something of this great land to the south. Although there are no records to confirm the facts, their trading junks and praos doubtless sailed within sight of its northern shores, and their ships' crews probably landed at one spot or another. But

the Western world did not learn about this land down under
until it was encountered by European explorers and adventurers.

The first vague facts about this southern continent were reported by Portuguese and Spanish explorers in the sixteenth century, as they charted their ways through unknown seas, seeking
new routes to the Spice Islands. Willem Janzoon of Amsterdam
must have come almost within sighting distance of the northern

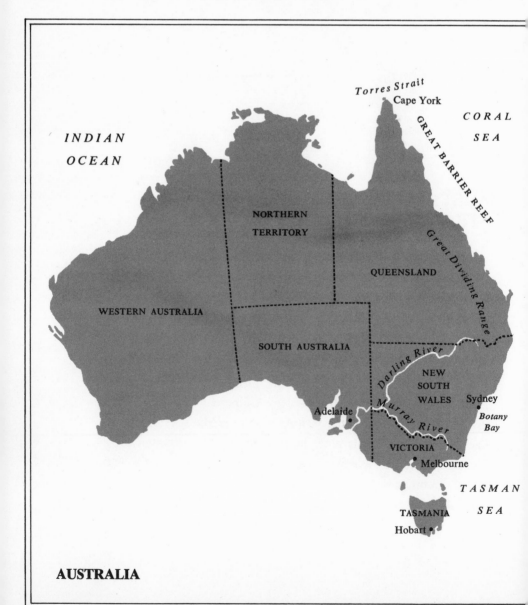

AUSTRALIA

coasts of Queensland in 1605, as he sailed "for the discovery of the land called Nova Guinea, which, it is said, afforded great store of gold." But he evidently found neither gold nor Australia. The next year the Spanish navigator, Luis de Torres, sailed through the narrow strait that now bears his name, between New Guinea and Australia, and from 1610 on various Dutch mariners sighted or touched on the western coast of Australia, which they called New Holland, as they sailed to the Spice Islands by way of Cape Horn and the Indian Ocean.

Early Exploration

In 1629, the Dutch vessel *Batavia,* under Captain François Pelsaert, was wrecked on Houtman Rocks, a group of small islands off the western coast of the continent. From that incident comes the first description of a member of the kangaroo family: "We found on these islands large numbers of a species of cats, which are very strange creatures; they are about the size of a hare, their head resembling the head of a civet-cat; the forepaws are very short. . . . Its two hind legs, on the contrary, are upwards of half an ell in length, and it walks on these only, on the flat of the heavy part of the leg, so that it does not run fast. Its tail is very long, like that of a long-tailed monkey; if it eats, it sits on its hind legs and clutches its food with its forepaws, just like a squirrel or monkey." The species that Pelsaert thus described was the dama wallaby, a small kangaroo still found on the islands today.

In 1642, Anton Van Dieman, governor general of the Dutch East Indies, sent Dutch mariner Abel Tasman on a voyage of exploration, the object being to take advantage of the west-wind belt and find a southern route to South America. Sailing westward from Batavia across the Indian Ocean, Tasman touched at Mauritius, then sailed southeast until he reached Tasmania, which he named Van Dieman's land in honor of the governor general. Later, he discovered New Zealand some one thousand miles farther east. Satisfied that a clear route to South America lay open across the Pacific from there, he turned north and returned to Batavia by passing to the north of New Guinea. Along the way he discovered the Tonga and Fiji Islands. In ten months Tasman had sailed completely around the continent of Australia without actually finding out much about it. In some measure he had charted the extent of the great southern continent, however, and had discovered Tasmania and New Zealand, as well as some remote and beautiful South Sea Islands.

Captain Cook Discovers Botany Bay

Coming along more than a century after Tasman, Captain James Cook, the famous English mariner and explorer, was the first European to explore and describe the eastern coast of Australia and to chart the coasts of New Zealand, eastern Australia, and New Guinea. Cook made three voyages to the Pacific between 1768 and 1778 before being killed in a fight on Hawaii.

In April, 1770, Captain Cook sailed to the east coast of Australia and anchored at Botany Bay. (Today the bay is surrounded by high-rise apartments in the suburbs of Sydney.) Cook and his men explored the green wilderness around the bay and marveled at the strange animals and plants they saw. Heading northward, Cook a few weeks later beached his ship *Endeavor* for repairs on the coast of the great peninsula that he christened Cape York. There he saw his first kangaroo: ". . . it was of a light mouse Colour and the full size of a Grey Hound. . . . Its progression is by Hopping or Jumping seven or eight feet at each hop upon its hind legs only. . . . It bears no sort of resemblance to any European animals I ever saw; it is said to bear much resemblance to the Jerboa, excepting in size, the Jerboa being no larger than a common rat."

On Cape York Captain Cook also saw and remarked upon

another animal, the flying fox, a huge bat with a foxlike face and a wingspread of three feet or more: "It was a most peculiar animal about the bigness of, and much like, a one-gallon keg. It was as black as the Devil, and had wings; indeed, I took it for the Devil, or I might easily have catched it, for it crawled very slowly through the grass."

Finally Cook reached the northern tip of the continent and Torres Strait. There, on August 22, 1770, he "hoisted the English colors, and in the name of His Majesty King George the Third took possession of the whole eastern coast," giving it the name New South Wales.

Cook had words of high praise for this new land he was claiming for England: "In this extensive country, it can never be doubted but what most sorts of grain, fruit, roots, etc. of every kind would flourish here were they once brought hither, planted, and cultivated by the hands of industry; and here are provender for more cattle, at all seasons of the year, than ever can be brought into the country."

Encouraged by Cook's glowing words, England began to settle the east coast of Australia in 1788, when a group of convicts debarked at Botany Bay. Each year thereafter the rich eastern and southern coasts received more settlers, and the transformation of Australia, after an isolation of many millions of years, was well launched. In 1803, Matthew Flinders chartered and surveyed much of the coastline of the continent, and the interior was finally explored in the nineteenth century.

Land of the Aborigines

The entire continent is smaller than the United States. Its northern tip, Cape York, thrusts into the tropics, just a few miles from the southern coast of New Guinea. Its eastern and southern coasts have a temperate climate, with rich grasslands and eucalyptus forests, a pleasant region, much like England in many ways. The eastern forests and farmlands rise into highlands and mountain ranges, separating the green coastal areas from the drier and more sparsely settled western half of the continent. The heartland of Australia is a forbidding desert, which endures long periods of drought and searing heat. Few men, animals, or plants inhabit this great area.

European settlers coming to Australia found that it was inhabited by slim, dark-skinned people who led a nomadic way of life and whose Stone Age culture sufficed their needs. Living intimately with nature, the aborigines left little mark upon the land, using what they found without changing it. ". . . in reality they are far more happy than we Europeans, being wholly unacquainted not only with the superfluous but with the necessary conveniences so much sought after in Europe," wrote Captain Cook approvingly in his journal. "They are happy in not knowing the use of them."

The aborigines are thought to have arrived in Australia from islands to the north some 20,000 to 30,000 years ago. There were probably no more than 400,000 of them when Europeans came to stay, less than 200 years ago. Today they have been reduced to 70,000 or less. "Wherever the European has trod," remarked Charles Darwin after his visit to Australia in 1836, "death seems to pursue the aboriginal."

Australia's Remarkable Wildlife

Most of the animals the Europeans found were quite different from those in other portions of the world. Australia had been separated from Asia near the end of the Age of Reptiles. Mammals were just getting their start at that ancient time, and primitive forms still dominated.

In Australia, primitive pouched mammals were the predominant forms at the time of Australia's separation from Asia, and the southern continent's long isolation from the rest of the world allowed these remarkable mammals to flourish and evolve without competition from more advanced forms. Specializing and adapting in many different ways, these pouched marsupials occupied all of the different ecological habitats that Australia had to offer.

Wolflike and catlike carnivorous marsupials took over the role of predators; kangaroos, wallabies, and a host of smaller forms became grazers and browsers; pouched moles, anteaters, mice, and rats appeared. "Australia may be regarded as the natural home of marsupials," remarks Australian naturalist, Ellis Troughton. "They come to us as a natural heritage from the past, born of our continent's age-old isolation, woven on the loom of evolution, and as characteristic of the land as are the birds, gumtrees, and wattles so beloved by Australians as emblematic of their country."

Along with the pouched mammals, two forms of even more primitive mammals survived—the egg-laying platypus and the echidna. The only advanced mammals already established in Australia when the aborigines arrived were bats and small rodents, which probably arrived on storm-driven logs or other floating platforms. The aborigines are thought to have brought with them the dingo, or wild dog. This advanced predator began immediately to make inroads on the defenseless native marsupials. But the dingo represented only the beginning.

Introduced Animals

When European settlers came to Australia less than two hundred years ago, they brought with them domestic stock and many kinds of Western plants, as well as such familiar wild animals of Europe as the rabbit, the fox, the stoat, and many others. The effect that these new species had on the native Australian fauna proved devastating. Many of the smaller marsupials disappeared even before they could be studied and described. As the zoologist W. K. Gregory observed in 1924: "Late in the eighteenth century there arrived in Australia by far the most destructive placental mammal the world has ever seen, *Homo sapiens,* variety *europaeus,* who has devastated the continent and is now completing the work of destruction."

Part of this devastation was the result of the unequal competition between the native pouched mammals and the more advanced placental mammals. Part was due to the wholesale destruction of the natural environment in many areas, almost wholly caused by modern man and the animals and plants he brought with him.

As Captain Cook had predicted, the land was good for stock, and sheep raising became the national industry. Millions of sheep changed the fertile grasslands to near deserts through overgrazing. And rabbits accelerated the process after their introduction to the continent in 1859.

Multiplying in incredible numbers in this new and virgin territory, with few of the natural checks and enemies that had kept them under control in Europe, rabbits were soon the scourge of the continent. In 1882, nine million rabbits were killed and their skins exported in efforts to control them; in 1927, some thirty million. Not until 1950 did an introduced viral disease, myxomatosis, provide a partial control.

Stockmen fought the rabbit fiercely—and they still do—for rabbits have contributed greatly to the devastation of the land. In Australia there is not enough grass to go around, when divided between sheep and rabbits—both of which overgraze the land—and native kangaroos, which have been cropping their share of the vegetation for millions of years without harm. Many stockmen kill off kangaroos as well as rabbits every chance they get. They also hunt the hated dingo, which they regard as a vicious sheep killer. More than $300 million have been spent in the dingo war so far, using guns, traps, poisons, and a 5000-mile fence has been erected across the continent in an effort to keep them out of the sheep country.

The real losers in all of these unequal struggles and sheep wars, however, have been the native flora and fauna.

DUCK-BILLED PLATYPUS
Ornithorhynchus anatinus

Recording his impressions of New South Wales in 1802, a pioneering Australian named Collins noted: ". . . an amphibious animal, of the mole species . . . has been lately found on the banks of a lake near the Hawkesbury . . . the most extraordinary circumstances observed in its structure was, its having, instead of the mouth of an animal, the upper and lower mandibles of a duck."

The early settlers called this curious creature a "duck-mole" or "water-mole." The aborigines referred to it as "mallangong." Today it is known as the duck-billed platypus.

The platypus has many other extraordinary features besides those mentioned by Collins. It is covered with thick velvety fur like a mole, has webbed feet like the otter, and shoulder bones

that osteologists liken to those of an alligator. The male of this remarkable species has a poison spur somewhat like a rattlesnake's fangs on each rear leg; the female lays eggs and suckles her young.

This paradoxical, believe-it-or-not mammal inhabits freshwater streams and lakes of eastern Australia and Tasmania. It digs elaborate burrows in stream banks, sleeping in them by day, and venturing out into the water at night to feed on crayfish, earthworms, tadpoles, and aquatic insects. After courtship and mating, the female lays her round white eggs—usually two in number—in an underground leaf nest and incubates them until they hatch some ten or twelve days later. The young platypuses usually do not venture out of the nest until they are nearly four months old.

Just reading a description of the platypus or looking at a stuffed specimen cannot give an adequate impression of the living animal. It has to be seen to be believed.

In 1798, the first platypus skin arrived at the British Museum in London. The next year the anatomist George Shaw described the animal and gave it the scientific name, *Platypus anatinus,* "flat-footed, like a duck." In 1800, the species was independently described by a German naturalist as *Ornithorhynchus paradoxus,* "the strange, bird-billed one." The scientific name used today is a combination of the first two: *Ornithorhynchus anatinus,* "with a bird-beak like a duck."

For many years after its discovery, discussion and argument persisted in scientific circles as to where this species belonged in the animal kingdom. In 1802, a complete specimen of the platypus was dissected by an English anatomist, Everard Home, who assigned it to a new class of animal intermediate between mammals, birds, and amphibians. To him it seemed to be neither fish, flesh, nor fowl. A French naturalist, Étienne Geoffroy Saint-

Hilaire, dissected a platypus and declared that it was an egg layer. Then a fellow countryman, Jean Baptiste Lamarck, declared that it was not a mammal because it lacked teats.

In 1824, a German anatomist discovered milk-producing glands in the species and assigned it without question to the mammals. But was it an egg layer, as many insisted? Anatomically it certainly seemed to be one, for its rectum and urogenital system opened into a common cloaca, as is true of reptiles and birds. But the crucial point as to whether it really laid eggs had never been finally settled to everyone's satisfaction.

In 1884, however, the English zoologist, W. H. Caldwell, actually collected eggs of the platypus and dispatched an exultant cablegram, "Monotremes oviparous, ovum microblastic," to the British Association for the Advancement of Science, which was then meeting in Montreal, Canada. The news evoked a minor sensation.

During the nineteenth century the platypus was hunted for its soft fur, which was used in the making of platypus rugs and robes. Its numbers dwindled in most of its range, and for a time it seemed doomed to extinction, along with many other Australian mammals. In recent years, however, the platypus has been rigidly protected, and for the foreseeable future its survival seems reasonably secure. One danger that must be guarded against is the pollution of its fresh-water environment with poisons like DDT and other deadly chlorinated hydrocarbon pesticides, as well as the phosphate contamination from farm fertilizers. The cumulative effect of pesticide poisons could affect the reproductive processes of the platypus just as adversely as it has affected those of the bald eagle, peregrine falcon, brown pelican, and many other wildlife species all over the world.

The first platypus ever seen outside its native habitat was brought to the New York Zoological Park in 1922 by the well-known animal dealer, Ellis Joseph. In spite of all-out efforts to keep it alive and healthy, this specimen lived only forty-seven days in the zoo.

David Fleay, an Australian naturalist and platypus enthusiast, kept one specimen alive and healthy at the Melbourne Zoo in 1937. During 1943 and 1944 he was successful in breeding platypuses in captivity at the Healesville Sanctuary in Australia, when he was the director, and subsequently raised a young platypus born there.

Buoyed by such progress in platypus keeping, the New York Zoological Society tried again, when David Fleay brought three platypuses to them in 1947. Two of them lived for more than ten years and were great favorites with the zoo-going public of New York.

In 1970, Australia placed a total ban on the export of any platypuses, so they are not likely to be seen anywhere now except in the Blue Mountain region of New South Wales. And even there the chances of seeing them are highly unlikely because of their elusive, nocturnal habits. No effort should be spared to insure the survival of the platypus, for its equal will never again be seen on earth.

KANGAROOS
Family Macropodidae

The best known of all the marsupials, kangaroos are the symbol of Australia—both of the continent and the nation. Their likeness is featured on coins and stamps and on the nation's coat of arms. Kangaroos are found only in Australia and New Guinea, and there they have evolved into many species of various sizes and habits to take advantage of different habitats. In size they range from the little rat kangaroo to the great gray, which stands five to seven feet high and weighs as much as two hundred pounds. Between these two forms are a host of others

of varying sizes and colors, known by such names as tree kangaroos, rock wallabies, and wallaroos. Altogether the family
Macropodidae includes fifty species or more. All of them have
the same general form, with enlarged hind feet (*Macropus* means
"big foot"), small forelimbs, and a long tail that acts as a
balancer when hopping or as a third foot when stopping to eat.

The best-known species—those recognized everywhere as
kangaroos—are the big ones: the red kangaroo of the interior
plains and ranching country; the several forms of the great
gray, or forester, kangaroo; and the Euro kangaroo, or wallaroo,
which lives in rocky country. These giants of the family have
been familiar sights in Australia ever since its settlement. The
mature male is called a buck, or boomer, the adult female is
known as a doe, immature females are called fliers, and baby
kangaroos are known as joeys. Most Australians view them
with toleration and affection, but not the ranchers and sheepmen. They consider kangaroos pests, rivals for valuable grass
and water needed by their domestic flocks.

red kangaroo

The settling of the country has affected the kangaroo family in two very different ways. Land clearing and the environmental changes brought about by ranching have worked against smaller species of kangaroos by depriving them of natural cover and food. The fox and other introduced predators have also reduced their numbers. But the clearing of land for ranching and the creation of artificial water holes in dry country has, in some instances, been advantageous to several of the larger kangaroos. The red kangaroo, for example, thrives in open country and, in fact, increased its population during the first half of the twentieth century.

As a result, most stockmen urge kangaroo control by any available means. Many hunters need no urging, however; they go after kangaroos for profit. The skins are used extensively in the manufacture of all sorts of leather products, and the soft fur is featured in children's toys and as souvenir trophies. Kangaroo meat is processed as pet food and is sometimes used for human consumption. Kangaroo-tail soup is still a popular Australian delicacy.

Because of these multiple onslaughts, Australia's annual kangaroo kill increased steadily, reaching a high of nearly two million annually during the 1950s and 1960s. For the past fifteen years between one and two million animals have been killed for export alone each year, the United States being the chief buyer of kangaroo products during that period.

Conservationists all over the world and many Australians have been justifiably alarmed by such slaughter. Controversy has long simmered between supporters of the kangaroo and commercial stockmen, the leather industry, and hunters. The United States market has provided hunters—both legal shooters and poachers—with the major economic incentive for kangaroo killing. Most of these hunters are equipped with jeeps, searchlights for night hunting, rifles with telescopic sights, and in many cases an enthusiastic disregard for regulations.

The uproar against the killing grew to such proportions by 1970 that stricter limits and controls were imposed. These laws reduced the legal take to approximately one million animals yearly. In answer to a call for an immediate five-year embargo on the export of kangaroo meat, the Australian Parliament also set up a Select Committee on Wildlife Conservation, which investigated the kill of the larger kangaroos. In November of 1971, this committee concluded that the only large species in danger was the Tasmanian form of the great gray kangaroo. Because this island form was being threatened by loss of habitat, it was afforded legal protection.

At this point several Australian wildlife-management organizations started to promote a philosophy of managing kangaroos and harvesting them for profit on a sustained yield basis. They claimed that the largest kangaroos have increased in numbers with improvements in their habitat since stocking with sheep began. Building on this base, they tried to convince farmers that kangaroos should be managed and cropped along with such domestic stock as sheep and cattle and that such harvesting would be economically worth their while. In accordance with that philosophy, the National Parks and Wildlife Foundation purchased a 10,700-acre ranch 370 miles northwest of Sydney, with the idea of raising kangaroos there as a food animal.

Meanwhile, rampant poaching continued and even increased. Criticism of Government policy became so great that in the spring of 1973 Australia banned the export of all kangaroo products and began a crackdown on illegal kills. Sheepmen opposed such a policy and fought back vigorously, claiming that kangaroo populations had increased greatly during 1973. The following year they proposed that a million animals should be killed by poisoning water holes. This poisoning program was never implemented. Best present estimates put the total number of big kangaroos in Australia at as many as twenty million animals. But how long can even such a large population stand an annual kill of one to two million—or more?

The whole history of the kangaroo question has been heavily overlaid with elements of human politics, prejudices, and profit motives, not only in Australia but also in the United States. In January, 1975, the United States Department of the Interior placed the red, the eastern gray, and the western gray kangaroos on their "threatened" list and banned the import of their products into the United States for commercial purposes. However, a loophole was left in the regulations. If Australia certified that any of its states had developed an effective sustained-yield program for kangaroos, skins from that state would be allowed into the United States. A little over a month later, Australia did lift its export ban in two states, allowing New South Wales to export 205,000 skins in 1975 and South Australia to export 80,000 skins. The United States Department of the Interior hastily announced that it had not received official Australian Government certificates to that effect. Meanwhile, the kill of kangaroos continues. Only time will tell what the fate of Australia's big kangaroos—and its small ones—will be.

WHITE-THROATED, OR PARMA, WALLABY
Macropus parma

An encouraging footnote to the subject of kangaroos is the story of the white-throated, or parma, wallaby. This little kangaroo, thought to be extinct for more than thirty years, has recently been rediscovered.

A handsome ten-pound animal with warm, reddish fur, a white cheek stripe, and a dark stripe on the neck, the white-throated wallaby originally inhabited coastal country of New

South Wales, but gradually it disappeared before settlement. By 1948 it had not been seen for many years and was presumed extinct. In 1965, however, a thriving population of the species was found on Kawau Island, a little speck of land off the north-west coast of North Island, New Zealand. It had been introduced onto Kawau about 1870 by Sir George Gray, an early governor of South Australia. At least two other kinds of wallabies had also been introduced to Kawau, and by 1965 the island populations of these animals was so dense that a campaign to control and lower their numbers was undertaken. In the course of the campaign a great many white-throated wallabies were killed before their true identity had been determined.

Since 1968, the species has been given official protection, and several controlled breeding colonies have been established as well. Recently the white-throated wallaby has also been found on the Australian mainland in a coastal region of northern New South Wales. Between 1966 and 1970 nearly four hundred specimens of this wallaby were exported to zoos all over the world.

HAIRY-NOSED WOMBAT
Lasiorhinus latifrons

Charting the strait between Australia and Tasmania at the end of the eighteenth century, explorers George Bass and Matthew Flinders observed some strange animals on several islands. Writing in 1801, Flinders remarked: "The new animal, called Wombat by the natives . . . has the appearance of a little bear. It eats grass and other vegetable substances, and its flesh something resembles tough mutton. The animal is about the size of a turnspit dog, but there is not too much meat upon it for three or four people to eat in a day."

This early account does not really shed much light on one of Australia's most interesting animals. The wombat is beaver-like in size and appearance, except that it is practically tailless. An exclusive vegetarian, it has teeth like those of a rodent, with a single pair of constantly growing incisor, or gnawing, teeth in each jaw. Equipped with powerful forelimbs and stout claws, it is an expert burrower and is notorious for digging lengthy tunnels and burrows. Like its arboreal relative the koala, the wombat has a backward-opening pouch—one with an entrance away from the head rather than toward it, as is true of kangaroos. It usually gives birth to just one young at a time.

The several species of wombats are usually divided into two groups: naked-nosed wombats that generally live in coastal country and hairy-nosed wombats that inhabit inland areas. At one time wombats could be found in the eastern part of the continent from northern Queensland to Victoria and South Australia, as well as in Tasmania. Today they have disappeared completely over vast stretches of former range and are threatened in their remaining areas.

Ranchers and stockmen destroy wombats because they compete with livestock for food. Also, their burrows provide convenient shelters for pestiferous rabbits, and the entrance holes make hazardous footing for livestock. As a consequence, naked-nose wombats are greatly reduced throughout their range; the Queensland hairy-nosed wombat is found in only one small area of mideastern Queensland, where it is now protected, and the southern hairy-nose wombat apparently survives only in a few isolated colonies in semiarid regions of South Australia.

As one step toward protecting this southern wombat, a 13,800-acre sheep station was purchased as a wombat reserve by the Chicago Zoological Society in 1972, with a grant from the Forest Park Foundation in Illinois. This fenced and patrolled reserve protects about two thousand wombats.

KOALA
Phascolarctos cinereus

With its soft, silver-gray fur, tufted ears, black patent-leather nose, and appealing teddy-bear look, the koala is a favorite animal not only with Australians but with people all over the world. But that has not always been the case. At one time the koala was hunted almost to extinction.

The first published account of this remarkable marsupial was printed in the *Sydney Gazette* in 1803, just a few months after this pioneering Australian newspaper started publication: "An animal whose species was never before found in the Colony is in the possession of his Excellency [Governor King, administrator of the colony of New South Wales]. When taken it had two pups, one of which died a few days since. This creature is somewhat larger than the Waumbut, and, although it might at first appearance be thought much to resemble it, nevertheless differs from that animal . . . the graveness of the visage . . . would seem to indicate a more than ordinary portion of animal sagacity, and the teeth resemble those of a rabbit. The surviving pup generally clings to the back of the mother, or is caressed with a serenity that appears peculiarly characteristic; it has a false belly like the apposum, and its food consists solely of gum leaves, in the choice of which it is excessively nice."

Overall this article was an accurate and discerning account of the koala. The "false belly" refers to the female's backward-facing pouch. The koala's generic name *Phascolarctos* comes from the Greek and means "bear with the leather bag." The mother koala carries her young in this pouch for several months until it ventures forth to be carried about piggyback as she climbs through the trees in search of just the right gum, or eucalyptus, leaves to eat.

The koala is very selective in its diet and eats the leaves of only a very few of the more than three hundred kinds of eucalyptus trees found in Australia. Furthermore, these leaves are eaten only after they have reached a certain stage of growth, when their chemical composition is just right. Young leaves and shoots, which may contain dangerously high levels of prussic acid, are not eaten. The koala has opposable toes that enable it to cling securely to a branch while it eats. Its cutting, or incisor, teeth are rodentlike and grow constantly. As a further adaptation, the species has cheek pouches in which it carries food.

Australia's first white settlers sometimes called the koala a "native bear," although it has no relationship to true bears. Others noted its resemblance to the ground-dwelling wombat. The two species have many similarities and very likely had a common ancestor, but the wombat stayed on the ground while the koala took to an arboreal life.

The common name koala is the aboriginal term for "no drink," for the animal is seldom if ever seen to take water. It evidently obtains enough moisture from the juice of the leaves it eats or possibly from drops of dew or rain on the leaves.

When it was first seen and described, the koala was a common animal in gum forests of eastern and southern Australia. As the country became settled, its numbers declined, partly because of land-clearing and forestry practices, but mainly because it was hunted for its soft coat, which was marketed as wombat in the fur industry.

The slaughter of koalas reached appalling heights in the early

years of the twentieth century, when hundreds of thousands—
sometimes millions—were killed each year for export. More than
two million koala skins were exported from Australia in 1920,
and by the end of that year only an estimated five hundred survived in the entire state of Victoria.

In 1923, 10,000 licensed Queensland hunters harvested over
one-half million skins. By 1927 the koala was in retreat everywhere, with Queensland having the only remaining sizable population. That state seemed determined to finish off the species,
however, with a declared open season that year, during which
600,000 koala skins were taken in one month, and a million
during the year. After that slaughter the eventual extinction of
the koala seemed inevitable.

By 1939, on the eve of World War II, the koala had disappeared in South Australia. It was reduced to perhaps 200 in
New South Wales and to about 1000 in Victoria. In Queensland
there were possibly as many as 10,000. The koala was nearly
gone.

Protection came just in time, however, and the species has
been zealously guarded since the war's end. A number of refuges
have been established for it in the four Australian states where
it originally lived. Today the koala is flourishing so well in some
of these states that overpopulation is becoming a problem. In
such areas, surplus animals are trapped and then reintroduced
into new reserves that have been established in their old territories.

In 1947, Ellis Troughton, an Australian mammalogist who
was one of the koala's greatest defenders, voiced the prevailing
opinion of his countrymen about the species: "May their numbers miraculously increase to browse peacefully in sheltered
forest reserves, together with many others of our fascinating
zoological heritage from the past, under a perpetual protection
which Australians owe them."

Troughton's wish for the koalas has been realized, but many other species in the land down under desperately need similar protection and help.

LEADBEATER'S POSSUM
Gymnobelideus leadbeateri

Australia boasts many different kinds of possums. Some have gliding membranes and bear an amazing resemblance to the North American flying squirrels. Others have long fluffy tails and look like tree squirrels, except for their more pointed noses. Leadbeater's possum, a small species about as large as a red squirrel, is one. Its general color is grayish brown, with a dark dorsal stripe from nape to tail and with lighter underparts. It was originally described from two specimens collected in the vicinity of the Bass River Valley of southeastern Victoria in 1867. Two additional specimens were taken in 1900 and 1909 respectively, and in 1931 a fifth mounted specimen was discovered that had been collected "many years before." From that date until 1961 these five musty museum specimens were the

only Leadbeater's possums known to exist anywhere in the world. For half a century the species had been presumed extinct.

In 1961, however, the species was rediscovered in the central highlands of Victoria by H. E. Wilkinson of the National Museum of Victoria. He found a whole colony of fifteen or twenty of them. Since then, the Mammal Survey Group of the Field Naturalists Club of Victoria has observed the species in a number of other areas. It is fully protected by law, and its foreseeable future looks bright.

Leadbeater's possum remained undiscovered for so long partly because of its secretive habits. A denizen of wild wooded country, it is both arboreal and nocturnal, and under even the best of circumstances it is seldom seen. In addition, since Australia was the last of all the continents to be settled, large areas of its mountainous forest lands—the natural habitat of Leadbeater's possum—are still relatively unexplored.

NUMBAT, OR BANDED ANTEATER
Myrmecobius fasciatus

"We also found a small and beautiful animal which appeared not to have been discovered before; its size was about that of a squirrel and its colour of a yellowish cast, with light and dark shaded stripes across the hinder parts of the back; its tongue was very long in proportion to its body, for which reason we supposed it was an anteater."

It was no true anteater that Ensign Robert Dale found as he explored western Australia in 1831, however, but a peculiar little marsupial known to the natives as the numbat. With a long, tapering snout and a slender tongue that may be extended for several inches, the numbat is specialized—as the South American anteaters are—for an ant or termite diet. They usually live in areas where there are many decayed trees and termite nests. Although the female has no pouch, she carries her young about with her for some time. Usually four in number, the young are for some weeks securely attached to their mother's nipples, which—as is true of other marsupials—become swollen within their mouths.

Taking shelter in hollow logs, numbats are frequent victims to brush fires and land-clearing projects. Introduced predators such as the dog and fox prey on these animals as well. As a result, numbats were one of the first marsupials to disappear when regions were opened up for settlement and development.

Originally this little beast ranged over scrub and forest country from the southern portions of western Australia to Victoria and New South Wales. Two races are recognized, the eastern subspecies being more reddish and with underparts that are tawny-colored instead of white. The western race is thought to be in no immediate danger, but the rusty eastern form is rare and threatened with extinction.

THYLACINE

Thylacinus cynocephalus

Very doglike in appearance, the thylacine is the largest meat-eating marsupial. Standing two feet high at the shoulder, it has a body about forty-five inches long and a twenty-inch tail. The coat of short brown hair is interrupted across the back and sides with sixteen dark stripes. Hunting alone or in pairs, the thylacine runs down its prey like a dog, seizing and killing it with its fang-like canine teeth. The newborn young are carried in the mother's backward-opening pouch. Later they are housed in an underground den.

Also known as the Tasmanian tiger because of its stripes, the thylacine has another common name, marsupial wolf, which suits it better. The scientific name means "pouched dog with a wolf head."

Fossil remains show that the thylacine once inhabited the Australian mainland. It disappeared from that continent many thousands of years ago, in all probability soon after the dingo, the Australian wild dog, invaded the continent. The dingo never reached Tasmania, however, and the thylacine survived there until modern times. When Europeans arrived in Tasmania in the nineteenth century, the thylacine was a common animal over much of the island. As the land became settled, the population of small native marsupials and rodents—the thylacine's natural prey—became scarcer; as a result, the pouched meat eaters turned to poultry and sheep, which were easy to kill.

The settlers fought the thylacine with guns, traps, and poisons. As early as 1840 the Van Diemen's Land Company offered a six-shilling bounty for every thylacine scalp brought in for collection. In 1888, the Government started paying a bounty of one pound sterling for every adult thylacine and ten shillings for every immature specimen. When the last Government bounty was paid in 1909, records showed that hunters had collected bounties on 2268 animals, but many more were probably killed. Thylacines were becoming uncommon by this time, and soon there was a further rapid decline in their numbers. Some people thought that this decline was caused by an epidemic disease such as distemper that swept through the wild population.

By the 1920s the thylacine was rare everywhere, and in 1930 a farmer shot the last wild specimen to be recorded for many years. The only specimen surviving in captivity died in 1934 in the Hobart Zoo in Tasmania. The Government gave belated protection to the species about that time, but it seemed to be gone.

The thylacine certainly appeared to be extinct, but during the next twenty or thirty years there were repeated rumors and unverified reports of sightings of the animal. Numerous scientists and amateurs searched for it, and the respected Australian scientist, David Fleay, reported finding its tracks in the 1940s. He did not find a specimen, however.

In 1961, a young male thylacine was killed at Sandy Cape on the west coast of Tasmania, proof that the animal still survived. Two years later tracks and droppings were found in another area, and in 1966 a thylacine lair showing signs of recent occupation was discovered. Early in the same year the Government set aside as a game reserve a total of 1,600,000 acres in the southwest district of Tasmania. Dogs, cats, and guns were prohibited in the area, and if any thylacines survived, some of them were sure to be in this wilderness refuge. The preserve also served to protect spiny anteaters, or echidnas, platypuses, and the rare Tasmanian ground parrot. Meanwhile, the search for proof of the survival of the thylacine continues, with group after group seeking to find, photograph, and study it. There have been several reputed sightings in recent years, but none by trained naturalists.

More than a century ago the eminent English naturalist and bird painter John Gould visited Tasmania and collected many zoological specimens there. Writing of the thylacine, he prophesied: "When the comparatively small island of Tasmania becomes more densely populated and its primitive forests are intersected with roads from the Eastern and Western coasts, the numbers of this singular animal will speedily diminish. Extermination will have full sway and it will then, like the wolf in England and Scotland, be recorded as an animal of the past." A remarkably clear-sighted judgment, it may yet be proven false with strict protective laws and expanded reserves.

Australia Today

Smallest of all the continents, Australia was the last to be discovered and is by far the most sparsely settled. About thirteen million people live there today, a mere handful as compared to other continents or to the total world population of nearly four billion people. The United States (exclusive of Alaska) is just slightly bigger than Australia but has a population of two hundred and ten million, about sixteen times as many as live on the continent down under. And such teeming countries as India and China have population densities that are many times greater.

In spite of Australia's sparse population and brief human history, its land and native wildlife have felt the deteriorating effects of modern man more severely in many areas than in practically any other region of the world. Most of the human population is concentrated in a pleasant temperate strip on the eastern and southern coasts. Man's effect on this region has, therefore, been intensified, and the forests and grasslands have borne the brunt of the mistreatment. The vast interior of the continent is too hot and arid to support a great deal of life, but marginal semiarid lands have been used far beyond their capacity. As a result of this misuse, they have deteriorated even more. Some people believe that the whole western two thirds of the continent, between the Darling River and the Indian Ocean, are on the verge of changing from merely arid to true desert land. In such dry areas, the effects of overgrazing and the impact on the native fauna of rabbits, dingoes, foxes, and other introduced animals are doubly devastating. One ecologist estimates that at least 18 species of Australian mammals and 13 birds have become extinct during the past 200 years. The true totals might well be larger. At present, at least 25 of Australia's 120 species of marsupials are considered to be in immediate danger of extinction. The populations of many others are also dwindling, and they may disappear within the next 50 years unless the current trend is reversed.

There are hopeful signs for wildlife in Australia, however, for the conservation consciousness of the nation has been raised in recent years. Many programs to protect and conserve wildlife are being put into effect, and additional nature reserves and parks are being created.

Possibilities also exist that some species long-considered extinct may still survive in remote and as yet little-explored areas. Two previously mentioned examples are the white-throated wallaby and the Leadbeater's possum. Another is the striped grass wren, a little bird that had not been seen since 1883 and had been thought to be extinct for nearly a century.

In 1973, however, a naturalist rediscovered it in scrub country of central New South Wales. In the same way, a naturalist in 1966 found a frisky pygmy possum in a ski hut on Mount Hotham in the Victorian Alps; after examination by experts, it proved to be a species that had previously been known only as a fossil. A flourishing colony of these little mountain possums was later found in Kosciusko National Park in New South Wales.

With regard to animals, it is a most remarkable fact, that so large an island . . . with varied stations, a fine climate, and land of all heights, from 14,000 feet downward, with the exception of a small rat, did not possess one indigenous animal.

Charles Darwin

8

NEW ZEALAND, LAND OF FLIGHTLESS BIRDS

Geologists believe that New Zealand has been isolated from all other lands for at least seventy million years. Until the last thousand years, it has been without human inhabitants. Roughly twelve hundred miles to the east of Australia and Tasmania, New Zealand is a rugged, mountainous land with numerous volcanoes, glaciers, and large areas of lush, forested wilderness. It consists of two main land masses—North Island and South Island, separated from each other by sixteen-mile-wide Cook Strait—with countless smaller islands scattered along their rugged coastlines.

Stretching over one thousand miles of ocean, from 35 to 48 degrees of south latitude, New Zealand has a pleasant, temperate climate. With hot springs and fertile valleys, North Island hints of the tropics; with snow-capped peaks, glaciers, and forbidding rocky coasts, South Island reaches toward polar seas.

Isolated for such a long period of time, New Zealand developed its own distinctive fauna. With no predatory animals to threaten them, many flightless birds evolved. Dominant among them were the moas, a group of ostrichlike birds that varied from

NEW ZEALAND

small, goose-sized species to giants twelve feet tall. There were no native mammals except two bats and perhaps a small rodent or two. These latter, however, may have arrived as stowaways with the first men who came to New Zealand.

Settlement

Man first came to New Zealand about one thousand years ago, when a few Polynesians landed, perhaps driven to the islands by chance when their outrigger canoes were blown off course during a storm. Not until about the year 1300, however, did the main invasion come. This time, as their descendants record it, a great fleet of Polynesian long canoes arrived at "the land under the long, white clouds," a colonizing force that was deliberately seeking a new home away from the crowded ancestral home islands to the east. These new arrivals were Maoris, a warlike and advanced group of Polynesians, who quickly defeated and assimilated the earlier inhabitants. They were well intrenched when Western man first found the islands some 300 years later.

The European discoverer of New Zealand was the Dutch explorer, Abel Tasman, who landed on the islands in 1642 and named them after one of the regions of his native Holland. Captain Cook explored the islands in 1769 and returned on several subsequent voyages. Once it was known, New Zealand became a popular place for both missionaries and whalers to visit. In the 1840s it became a crown colony of the British Empire, but not without prolonged and determined opposition from the proud Maoris, who resented this modern invasion of their land. From 1861 until 1871 the Maoris fought the British invaders, often very effectively. Superior arms finally won out, but the Maoris were granted a considerable degree of autonomy.

As had happened in Australia, the exotic animals introduced by white settlers flourished in New Zealand—in many cases far too well. Rabbits multipled at an amazing rate, and wars of extermination were quickly declared against them. The European red deer was introduced in mid-nineteenth century, and many other antlered species soon followed—North American white-tailed deer and wapiti, English fallow deer, Asiatic sika deer, and various others. The deer flourished in the virgin lands, and for the past forty years or more some species have been so abundant that the Government has had to employ professional hunters and poisoners to keep them under control.

Rabbits, deer, sheep, and other introduced animals have caused extensive environmental damage in New Zealand, and their effect on native animals, especially the flightless birds, has been devastating. Man alone, however, was probably responsible for the disappearance of the moas.

MOAS
Family Dinornithidae

The moas are known today only by their bones and bits of other, mostly fossilized, remains. To date, more than twenty different species have been described and named. A number of them were still living in New Zealand when the Polynesians first came to the islands, and several forms may even have survived until the close of the eighteenth century. It is quite safe to say that man—the Maoris in this particular instance—caused this unique family of birds to disappear when it did. White explorers and settlers first learned about moas only through stories told to them by Maoris. Later they began to uncover more tangible proof of the birds' existence.

In 1839, an English traveler in New Zealand obtained the thigh bone of a huge creature, which he sent to the English anatomist, Richard Owen. Upon first examining it, Owen thought it was merely an ox bone. After more careful study, he determined that it had come from a huge ostrichlike bird. At about

great moa

this time two missionaries sent Owen a box full of similar bones.

After much study the noted anatomist described the birds from which the bones had come and gave them the generic name *Dinornis,* or "terrible bird." He also determined that at least five different forms were represented by the remains he had examined.

Between 1847 and 1850, Walter Mantell, a New Zealand Government official whose father was a noted geologist and paleontologist, collected over 1000 moa bones, bone fragments, and pieces of eggshell during extensive travels about the country. He sent the material to England for further examination and classification.

Various studies since that time have shown that the moas comprised more than twenty different forms. In 1949, excavations in Pyramid Valley, a swampy area some 100 miles from the northeast coast of South Island, unearthed virtually complete skeletons of about 140 specimens. At least a third were remains of the great moa *(Dinornis maximus),* which stood twelve feet tall. Pollen-dating methods demonstrated that the birds had been mired in the swamp over a period of many centuries, starting about A.D. 500. Sophisticated carbon-14 dating of the stomach contents of some of the largest remains showed an age of about 670 years. In other words, the great moa evidently survived until at least the year 1300, at about which time the legendary great fleet of the Maoris arrived in New Zealand.

Climatic changes may have been a contributing factor in the disappearance of the moas, but most students believe that man was the primary agent of extermination. The Maoris hunted the big flightless birds for food and had evidently killed most of them by the time Captain Cook visited New Zealand in the last quarter of the eighteenth century. A few moas may have survived until that time, however.

In 1844, an old Maori named Haumatangi came forward when questioned to say that he remembered Captain Cook's second visit in 1773. He further claimed that the last moa in his part of New Zealand had been seen just two years before Cook's visit. Another venerable native, one Kawana Paipai, said that when he was a boy—about 1790—he had actually taken part in moa hunts. The Maori hunters, he related, surrounded the defenseless birds and killed them with spears.

Further evidence of the existence of moas until comparatively recent times was uncovered in 1859, when a group of miners discovered a Maori tomb in which sat a complete human skeleton holding in its cupped finger bones an enormous moa egg, ten inches long by nearly eight inches in diameter.

One of the most tantalizing moa reports was recounted by Sir George Gray, governor of New Zealand in 1868. He declared that the natives had told him of the recent killing of a small moa, "describing with much spirit its capture out of a drove of six or seven." Were the natives telling the truth, or merely embroidering a tall tale about the killing of some flightless bird in order to please the governor? One is inclined to think that the latter is the case. Strong evidence points to the probability of a few moas still surviving to the latter years of the eighteenth century. Possibly a few may have survived in hidden wilderness areas for another seventy-five years or more, as the story of the supposedly extinct takahé clearly shows.

TAKAHÉ
Notornis mantelli

The takahé is a chicken-sized, flightless rail with thick scarlet legs, a short, blunt scarlet bill, and plumage that gleams iridescent blue on the breast and metallic green on the back and rump. Today the total wild population—an estimated two to three hundred birds—lives in a few isolated valleys in the Murchison Mountains of Fiordland, in the southwestern section of South Island. The takahé, like the moas, was first described from bones. Those takahé bones were collected by Walter Mantell, the same man who had collected so many moa bones. As he had done with the moa bones, Mantell forwarded the takahé remains to England.

Mantell had found his takahé bones near the mouth of the Waingongoro River in southern Taranaki, North Island, in 1847. After packing them up, he sent them to his geologist father in London, with the notation that these bones must be those of the bird known by the Maoris on North Island as the moho and by South Island Maoris as the takahé. Richard Owen agreed and named this supposedly extinct bird *Notornis mantelli,* after its finder.

Before long, however, a live takahé turned up. A group of seal hunters were camped in Dusky Sound, South Island, in 1849, when their dog brought in a large bird, which they promptly dispatched and ate. They did save its skin and skeleton, however, which were eventually deposited in the British Museum. Two years later a second specimen was caught in Thompson Sound, South Island. It too ended up in the British Museum.

Nearly twenty years passed before a third takahé was collected, in 1879. This specimen was sold at auction, with the Dresden Museum in Germany being the high bidder. A fourth was taken in 1898. The New Zealand Government finally bestirred itself to purchase this one for the Otago Museum on South Island.

Four museum specimens had been collected during a span of forty-nine years, hardly an indication that the takahé was a widespread or thriving species. No other living specimens turned up during the next half century, and the takahé was relegated to the extinct category. Unverified rumors and reports of the living bird continued to circulate, however, and there were a few bird watchers who still had hopes of finding living birds.

Dr. Geoffrey Orbell of Invercargill, South Island, was one. An enthusiastic amateur ornithologist, he followed up to the best of his ability every takahé report that came to him and undertook numerous trips to search for the bird in likely territory. In 1948, his efforts were finally crowned with success. At that time he rediscovered the living species in a small, hidden valley near Lake Te Anau, Fiordland: not just one specimen, but a whole colony of them. On one trip to the area, he netted two birds and took photographs before releasing them.

Upon hearing the news, the New Zealand Government immediately closed a huge area of some 435,000 acres as a protected sanctuary for the birds. Subsequent field investigation indicated that at least twenty breeding individuals were in the area, and perhaps forty to sixty nonbreeding birds. Today they are strictly protected, and a careful watch is kept over them. The total population is estimated at between two and three hundred birds living in eight small valleys within the protected area.

At one time, the takahé's range extended over suitable habitat in both North and South Islands where snow tussock grass—its principal food plant—grows. A slow breeder, the takahé constructs a bulky ground nest in which one or two eggs are laid. Only one usually hatches. The fuzzy black chick eats insects brought by the parent birds and takes three to four years to mature.

With a tiny, relict population, the takahé's toehold on survival is precarious. Climatic changes and severe winters probably account for some of the decline, but hunting by man and introduced predators helped to reduce the population, too. Indeed, dogs captured at least two of the first four living specimens that were taken, which ended up in museum collections.

In 1958, in an experimental program to breed the birds in captivity, four captured takahés and a few eggs were transported to the Mount Bruce Native Bird Reserve, near Masterson, North Island. This action created great controversy among New Zealand birders, just as the taking of whooping-crane eggs for the same purpose did in the United States. The takahé breeding program produced no positive results for a number of years.

Captive birds did lay a total of sixteen eggs between 1966 and 1969, but none of them proved to be fertile. On Christmas day, 1972, the station reported its first success: two takahé chicks hatched at the reserve that day, the first of the species ever bred in captivity. Although they did not survive, their hatching did demonstrate the possibility of successful captive breeding and rearing in the future.

KAKAPO
Strigops habroptilus

Another bird that threatens to follow the path of the moas is the kakapo, or owl parrot, a species that once ranged widely over both of New Zealand's main islands. A fairly large bird that sometimes measures as much as two feet in length, the kakapo has colors that provide excellent camouflage for a species that spends most of its time on the ground. Its back and wings are mossy green, interrupted with brown and black mottling; the underparts are yellowish green. Hiding in rock crevices during the day, the kakapo comes out at night to feed on berries,

buds, and other vegetation. Its common name comes from the Maori, and means "parrot (kaka) of the night (po)."

Although flightless for all practical purposes, the kakapo does climb trees in search of food and has been observed "flying" earthward after feeding, using its stubby degenerate wings to help cushion its fall. It builds its nest in an underground burrow and lays its two to four large white eggs in January or February, which is summer in New Zealand.

A near-flightless species, the kakapo was easy prey for such introduced predators as dogs, cats, rats, and weasels. The activities of European settlers worked against it, too. They have reduced the original forest habitat of the kakapo to a quarter of its original extent; in addition, many of them used to kill it for sport.

Since 1930, the species has disappeared entirely from North Island, and today it is found only in a few scattered areas of western Fiordland on South Island. One of the world's rarest species, its total population is probably fewer than one hundred birds.

In the past, bird fanciers who kept kakapos in captivity rated the species very highly as a pet. One enthusiast noted that it is as affectionate as a dog and playful as a kitten.

STEPHEN ISLAND WREN
Xenicus lyalli

A tiny, rock-ribbed speck of land in Cook Strait just off the northeastern tip of South Island, Stephen Island is distinguished from many similar small islands by its lighthouse. One of the keepers of that light brought a cat with him in 1894, presumably to keep him company on his lonely outpost. The cat, like cats anywhere, stalked and hunted any small animals that it could spot among the barren rocks. What it found, pounced upon, and brought back to its master was a succession of little, short-tailed

birds with light-colored breasts and mottled brown feathers on their backs.

They were peculiar-looking specimens, and the interested lighthouse keeper preserved a dozen or so of them. Eventually they were sent to England and Europe, where ornithologists studied them and reported that they were a hitherto unknown and undescribed species. Meanwhile, no more specimens were taken. The cat had evidently gotten them all.

The Stephen Island wren was said to be a seminocturnal bird that skulked among the rocks for its food. Adapted to living where there was no threat from native predators, it was never seen to fly. Indeed, it may have been the only known perching bird that was flightless. It was also the only known species to have been rendered extinct by a single cat.

TUATARA
Sphenodon punctatus

During Triassic times, roughly 200 to 170 million years ago, a distinct group of reptiles, the order Rhynchocephalia, or "beak-heads," flourished throughout much of the world. As determined from fossil remains, more than forty different kinds of beak-head lived in Eurasia, Africa, and South America at that time. During the next hundred million years—the prime of the great dinosaurs—the beak-heads gradually declined. Finally they disappeared everywhere, except for one small but very hardy and enduring species, the tuatara. Scientists today view the tuatara as the sole surviving representative of one of the five main divisions of living reptiles. The others are the crocodilians, the turtles, the lizards, and the snakes.

Until the mid-nineteenth century, scientists had thought that the order Rhynchocephalia had been extinct for 100 million years or more. They were wrong, as they found out when the tuatara was discovered and described.

The species received its scientific name from John Edward Gray, an English zoologist, who described a specimen received at the British Museum in 1831. Gray thought that he was merely describing a new kind of lizard from far-off New Zealand. On further examination, his successor, Dr. Albert Gunther, recognized that he was examining a reptilian missing link, or living fossil, that possessed many unique peculiarities in its anatomy.

Anyone looking at a tuatara would consider it to be a typical lizard. Ranging from twenty to twenty-six inches in length, the adult has a covering of nonoverlapping, greenish brown scales, spattered with darker green and yellow spots; a crest of soft white spines runs down the head and back. Tuatara, the original Maori name, means "peaks on the back."

Although the tuatara superficially resembles a lizard, it has a number of distinct peculiarities that separate it from this better-known reptilian group. Unlike true lizards, the tuatara has an additional bone in its skull. The male has no intromittant sex organ, such as true lizards and snakes possess. The tuatara is equipped, however, (as are many lizards) with a third, or parietal, eye on the top of its head; this eye has a rudimentary lens, retina, and optic nerve, and it can probably differentiate only between light and dark. The tuatara is also equipped with a nictitating membrane, such as birds have, which can sweep over its true eyes and protect them.

When Europeans first came to New Zealand, this strange reptile lived on both North and South Islands. The white settlers brought pigs and goats and dogs with them, however, and these animals no doubt contributed to the quick disappearance of the species on the main islands. Some scientists believe that climatic changes and the Maoris also helped to eradicate it. Whatever the cause, tuataras had disappeared from the New Zealand main islands by 1850. Today they are found only on some twenty small coastal islands—one group of them lying off the coast of North Islands between North Cape and East Cape, and another group situated in Cook Strait.

On these small rocky islands the tuatara shelters in holes and burrows dug by petrels, shearwaters, and other oceanic birds. Almost entirely nocturnal, it ventures out at night to feed on insects, earthworms, and other small animals. During the New Zealand winter (our summer) it hibernates in the burrow. The petrels return to their burrows when warm weather comes and share them rather amicably with the tuataras. In October and November—springtime in New Zealand—the female tuatara lays eight to fifteen eggs in a shallow burrow, covering them with leaves and earth. She takes no further notice of them, and the eggs hatch some twelve to fifteen months later.

Hatching from a soft white egg, the six-inch-long baby tuatara is a delicate chocolate brown in color, with gray and white stripes. Although much more active than adults, the young develop slowly and may take twenty years to reach maturity. The life-span is lengthy, perhaps as much as one hundred years or more.

Today New Zealanders recognize the tuatara for the fascinating creature that it is and protect it. All of the islands upon which it lives are uninhabited and can only be visited with a special permit. The handling or taking of any specimens is also strictly regulated. Particular care is taken to ensure that no exotic animals such as rodents, dogs, cats, or goats are introduced into the tuatara's limited and delicately structured environment.

Under such protection, the tuatara still lives in peace on its restricted island habitat. On Stephen Island, tuataras blink at the entrance of their burrows, within sight of the lighthouse. In total, an estimated ten thousand or more of them still survive today, living fossils that trace their heritage back at least to the time of the dinosaurs.

Other Endangered Species

Some authorities estimate that over forty birds have become extinct on New Zealand and nearby islands since the Polynesians first settled on the main islands about a thousand years ago. A large number of them, of course, were the flightless moas. Others were two flightless geese, two ducks, a swan, several flightless rails, and many passerines, or perching birds. At least nine birds, the authorities add, have been exterminated since Europeans invaded the land two hundred years ago. Among them are the New Zealand quail, the New Zealand fruit pigeon, the North Island laughing owl, and the huia—a species among which the male had a short, starling-like bill while that of the female was long and curved.

The list of surviving birds that are considered to be threatened with extinction is lengthy. Fortunately, New Zealanders have come to appreciate their unique fauna and are today making strenuous efforts to save the endangered forms. Many reserves have been established, and biologists of the New Zealand Wildlife Service are attempting to propagate the takahé and other species.

Man's attitude toward nature is today critically important simply because we have now acquired a fateful power to alter and destroy nature. But man is a part of nature and his war against nature is inevitably a war against himself. Rachel Carson

9

WHAT IS THE FUTURE FOR WILDLIFE?

The preceding chapters look at what has happened—as well as what *is* happening—to the land and wildlife of the Old World. Man is exerting the same destructive forces on his environment and fellow living creatures in the New World and in the earth's oceans as well. Today thousands of different animals are heading toward extinction and will disappear unless the harmful effects of man's activities can be reversed.

"Rarity is the attribute of a vast number of species of all classes in all countries," Charles Darwin observed more than a century ago in his classic book, *The Origin of Species.* "If we ask ourselves why this or that species is rare, we can answer that something is unfavorable in its condition of life: but what that something is, we can hardly ever tell." The first part of that

261

statement is as true today as it was when Darwin wrote it, but not the last part. Today we can almost without exception tell what the unfavorable factors are, and in practically every case they are the result of human activities.

As the number of people in the world increase, the results become ever more marked. Wildlife disappears at an ever more rapid rate, and the overall quality of human life decreases. A few industrialized nations may be living well for the moment, but only at a high cost to all other countries and to planet Earth itself.

The declining fortunes of much of the earth's wildlife as a result of environmental destruction could serve as a clear indication of what lies in store for us if we do not alter our attitudes and ways. "Don't dismiss our extermination of passenger pigeons and Carolina parakeets by saying that extinction has always gone on," warns biologist Daniel L. McKinley. "If anything is to be learned it is that extinction comes to species that don't change their ways. Can we? Besides, if we can't save whooping cranes or snow leopards, how can we save ourselves?"

The passenger pigeon, the Carolina parakeet, the dodo, and most of the other recently extinct animals disappeared because they were unable to change their ways when faced with harmful conditions brought about by human beings. The sands of natural evolution grind exceedingly slow, and none of the higher animals, *except* man, can adapt quickly to extensive changes in their environment. Human beings are unique in the fact that they *can* change their ways quickly when the need arises. The important questions are: *will* we, and will we change before it is too late?

A Rising Ecological Conscience

There is recent and encouraging evidence that we are, at last, beginning to recognize the seriousness of our situation and starting to do something about it. Most of the highly developed nations, for example, are making substantial—although usually insufficient—efforts to deal with the problems of increasing population. Even so, another seventy-five years or more will pass before most of them, even if they make an all-out effort, can achieve zero population growth. Meanwhile, the populations of developing nations will continue to increase—and starve.

One horn of the dilemma is the fact that the highly industrialized nations represent only about a third of earth's human population, but that one third is using up nearly 90 percent of the planet's resources, and in the process are creating much of the basic problem. However late, these advanced nations are beginning to realize that they bear a great deal of the responsibility for the pollution and environmental destruction that occurs around the world and that they must take the lead in stopping such activities. Many nations are enacting legislation designed to protect their lands and wildlife; many are establishing new wilderness preserves and parks within their borders.

In 1972, the United Nations World Conference on the Human Environment was convened at Stockholm, at which the multiple problems of habitat deterioration, pollution, and dwindling resources were brought to the consciousness of all nations. Other United Nations conferences—on population, on food, and on the resources of the sea—soon followed.

In the spring of 1973, some eighty nations met in Washington, D.C., to draft a convention to control international trade in endangered species of wildlife. Overall, the conference listed 178 species of mammals, 113 birds, 44 reptiles, and a number of other animals presently threatened with extinction. Under the terms of the agreement all commercial traffic in these species was banned, worldwide. Another 239 kinds of animals were categorized as threatened to a lesser extent, which meant that products of these animals could be bought and sold and traded among nations only under a permit system; further, the status of these species was to be carefully and constantly monitored. These terms were put into effect worldwide in July, 1975, after the required number of nations had ratified them.

Also in 1973, as a result of the United Nations Conference on the Human Environment the previous year, an ongoing United Nations Environmental Program was established, with headquarters in Nairobi, Kenya. There, environmental activities of member nations are examined and coordinated, supervised under a global monitoring system called Earthwatch.

Attitudes toward killing animals merely for sport are undergoing significant changes in many nations, and the practice of wildlife management is perceptibly shifting away from the aim of only helping game species to the concept of managing areas for the general benefit of all the wildlife species.

All such trends are cause for some optimism about the future of endangered wildlife—and for mankind's future as well. So are the recent scientific breakthroughs, and the new concepts and techniques that are being used to help an increasing number of threatened species.

New Knowledge, New Techniques

Many of the current practices—both old and new—used to help endangered wildlife have been mentioned in previous pages. Species as different as the ibex, the rhinoceros, and the koala are being captured and successfully transplanted from areas of concentration to regions where they formerly lived but had long since disappeared. The technique of shooting large animals such as the rhinoceros with tranquilizer darts that temporarily immobilize them makes transporting them without danger possible. Birds such as the European white stork, the peregrine falcon, and the osprey have been aided by the erection of nesting platforms, the banding of young to check local movements and migration patterns, and the transfer of eggs from one area to another in order to establish new breeding colonies. Tiny radio transmitters are sometimes fastened on captured animals—like bears, falcons, and alligators—in order to monitor and map their movements after release. Skilled behavioral studies, such as those conducted by George Schaller and Dian Fossey on the gorilla, have shed new light on how endangered species may be helped. Survival Centers have been established for some animals—the orangutan, for example—enabling captive specimens to be reintroduced to life in the wild gradually.

The science of breeding wild animals in captivity has made great advances in recent years. Species such as Père David's deer and the European bison survive today only because they were kept and protected in captive herds for many years. The Arabian oryx has some hope for the future only because similar methods, reinforced by modern veterinary science and improved methods of managing wild animals in captivity, are being utilized in its behalf. Careful breeding records and stud books are kept for a number of threatened species with captive groups in zoos and protected reserves all over the world. A few groups of animals are propagated in special breeding centers established just for them. The Ornamental Pheasant Trust and the Wildfowl Trust, both in England, are two examples. A number of leading zoological parks—London, San Diego, New York, and Washington among them—have established or are in the process of establishing huge natural areas covering many hundreds of acres, where endangered species can live and propagate under simulated natural conditions. Various zoos and animal study centers are also working to perfect techniques for breeding threatened species by artificial insemination. Commercial wild-animal farms successfully keep and breed such diverse species as African antelopes, kangaroos, crocodiles, and green turtles.

Any and all of these captive-breeding programs are most worthwhile when they hold forth the eventual possibility of re-introducing specimens to the wild under favorable conditions.

An Endangered Wildlife Research Program

As part of its work, the United States Fish and Wildlife Service maintains an Endangered Wildlife Research Program at its Patuxent Wildlife Research Center in Laurel, Maryland. There all kinds of new techniques for helping endangered species are developed and tested. Best known, perhaps, is the whooping-crane project, which has been going on for nearly ten years and which tests and utilizes many innovative techniques that may eventually be used to help a number of threatened species.

The United States Fish and Wildlife Service has recently established Recovery Teams of experts to develop programs in-dividually tailored to help a number of endangered species in the United States. Similar teams and dedicated individuals are studying threatened wildlife in many countries as well. Backing up all of these efforts are numerous conservation and wildlife organizations throughout the world.

All of these activities clearly demonstrate a marked shift in attitudes toward wildlife and the environment. "Power over life must be balanced by a reverence for life," Anne Morrow Lind-bergh has declared. ". . . and not simply life of man—life of animals, birds, butterflies, trees, flowers, crops. All life is linked. This is what makes up the 'good earth.' "

Concerned people everywhere hope that such attitudes and programs will become stronger day by day and year by year. They do not want a future in which generations will look back at the last quarter of the twentieth century and say, "There were still tigers and rhinoceroses and gorillas living in the wild in those days. But the people living then allowed them to be killed off;

all that remains to remind us of them are a few museum specimens."

Rather let us hope that they will be able to say, "Our earth is
alive and well, and we share it with all God's creatures. Perhaps
we never will see a platypus or a tiger in the wild, but at least
we know that they are there."

SELECTED BIBLIOGRAPHY

Publications of the International Union for the Conservation
of Nature and Natural Resources (IUCN), particularly the Red
Data Books on endangered species, and the Bulletins, have been
very helpful references in the preparation of this work. Among
the most useful magazines and periodicals have been the following: *Animal Kingdom* (New York Zoological Society); *Audubon*
(National Audubon Society); *Defenders* (Defenders of Wildlife); *International Wildlife* (National Wildlife Federation); *National Geographic* (National Geographic Society); *Natural History* (American Museum of Natural History); *Oryx* (Fauna
Preservation Society); and *Smithsonian* (The Smithsonian
Institution).

In Section I of this bibliography, I am listing for each chap-

269

ter selected books and articles that should be of especial interest to the reader who wishes to pursue a particular subject further. Section II lists a few selected titles on (1) exploration and discovery in the Old World; (2) man's effect on land and wildlife of all continents.

SECTION I

1   Man's Rise to Dominance
Becker, Carl L., and Duncalf, Frederic, *Story of Civilization*. New York: Silver Burdett Company, 1944.

Golding, William, *The Inheritors*. New York: Harcourt Brace Jovanovich, Inc., 1962. (A powerful fictional re-creation of primitive man.)

Hermann, Paul, *Conquest by Man*. New York: Harper & Brothers, 1954.

Howell, F. Clark, and the Editors of *Life, Early Man*. New York: Time, Inc., 1965.

McNeill, William H., *The Rise of the West*. Chicago: The University of Chicago Press, 1963.

Osborn, Fairfield, *Our Plundered Planet*. Boston: Little, Brown & Company, 1948.

Romer, Alfred S., *The Vertebrate Story*. Chicago: The University of Chicago Press, 1959.

2   Europe, Cradle of Western Civilization
Bourlière, François, and the Editors of *Life, The Land and Wildlife of Eurasia*. New York: Time, Inc., 1964.

Curry-Lindahl, Kai, *Europe: A Natural History*. New York: Random House, Inc., 1964.

Jennison, George, *Animals for Show and Pleasure in Ancient Rome*. Manchester: Manchester University Press, 1937.

Ley, Willy, *Exotic Zoology*. New York: The Viking Press, 1962.

(Account of the woolly mammoth and other wildlife species.)

Murray, Marion, *Circus! From Rome to Ringling*. New York: Appleton-Century-Crofts, Inc., 1956.

3   Asia, the Immense Land

Durant, Will, *The Story of Civilization, Vol. I, Our Oriental Heritage*. New York: Simon & Schuster, Inc., 1954.

Fox, Helen M., ed. and trans., *Abbé David's Diary, Being an Account of the French Naturalist's Journeys and Observations in China in the Years 1866 to 1869*. Cambridge: Harvard University Press, 1949.

Perry, Richard, *The World of the Giant Panda*. New York: Taplinger Publishing Company, 1969.

Pfeffer, Pierre, *Asia: A Natural History*. New York: Random House, Inc., 1968.

Polo, Marco, *The Book of Marco Polo*. New York: Grosset & Dunlap Universal Library, n.d.

Ripley, S. Dillon, and the Editors of *Life, The Land and Wildlife of Tropical Asia*. New York: Time, Inc., 1964.

Schaller, George B., *A Naturalist in South Asia*. A New York Zoological Society Report, Spring, 1971.

————, *The Deer and the Tiger*. Chicago: The University of Chicago Press, 1967.

Sheldon, William G., *The Wilderness Home of the Giant Panda*. Amherst: The University of Massachusetts Press, 1975.

Singh, Arjan, *Tiger Haven,* John Moorhead, ed. New York: Harper & Row, Publishers, 1973.

4   Africa, Land of the Last Great Herds

Bridges, William, "An Okapi Comes to the Zoological Park." *Animal Kingdom,* Vol. 40, No. 5, September-October, 1937.

Brown, Leslie, *Africa: A Natural History*. New York: Random House, Inc., 1965. (Includes material on Madagascar.)

Carr, Archie, and the Editors of *Life, The Land and Wildlife of*

Africa. New York: Time, Inc. 1964. (Includes material on Madagascar.)

Chapin, James P., "How the Congo Peacock Was Discovered." *Animal Kingdom,* Vol. 51, No. 6, May-June, 1948.

Cloudsley-Thompson, J. L., *Animal Twilight: Man and Game in East Africa.* London: G. T. Foulis & Co., Ltd., 1967.

Du Chaillu, Paul B., *Explorations and Adventures in Central Africa.* New York: Harper & Brothers, 1861.

Fisher, Alan C., Jr., "African Wildlife, Man's Threatened Legacy." *National Geographic,* Vol. 141, No. 2, February, 1972.

Fossey, Dian, "Making Friends with Mountain Gorillas." *National Geographic,* Vol. 137, No. 1, January, 1970.

————, "More Years with Mountain Gorillas." *National Geographic,* Vol. 140, No. 4, October, 1971.

Guggisberg, C. A. W., *Crocodiles, Their Natural History, Folklore and Conservation.* Harrisburg: Stackpole Books, 1972.

Lang, Herbert, "In Quest of the Rare Okapi." *Animal Kingdom,* Vol. 21, No. 3, May, 1918.

Leakey, Louis S. B., *Animals of East Africa.* Washington, D.C.: National Geographic Society, 1969.

Matthiessen, Peter, *The Tree Where Man Was Born;* Porter, Eliot, *The African Experience.* New York: E. P. Dutton & Company, Inc., 1972.

Moorhead, Alan, *No Room in the Ark.* New York: Harper & Row, Publishers, 1959.

————, *The White Nile.* New York: Harper & Row, Publishers, 1971.

Schaller, George, *The Year of the Gorilla.* Chicago: University of Chicago Press, 1964.

5   Madagascar and Islands of the Indian Ocean

Ley, Willy, *The Lungfish and the Unicorn: An Excursion into Romantic Zoology.* New York: Modern Age Books, 1941.

(Account of the dodo and other wildlife species.)

Marden, Luis, "Madagascar, Island at the End of the Earth." *National Geographic,* Vol. 132, No. 4, October, 1967.

McNulty, Faith, "Madagascar's Endangered Wildlife." *Defenders of Wildlife,* Vol. 50, No. 2, April, 1975. (A special issue on Madagascar.)

Tattersall, Ian, "Of Lemurs and Men." *Natural History,* Vol. 81, No. 3, March, 1972.

Topsell, Edward, *The Fowles of Heauen; or History of Birdes.* Thomas P. Harrison and F. David Hoeniger, eds. Austin: The University of Texas Press, 1972. (Topsell's manuscript of his translation and alphabetic abridgement of Aldrovandi's *Ornothologiae,* covering A-C; issued in 1599, 1600, and 1603.)

Wetmore, Alexander, "Re-creating Madagascar's Giant Extinct Bird." *National Geographic,* Vol. 132, No. 4, October, 1967.

6   The Malay Archipelago

Galdikas-Brindamour, Biruté, "Orangutans, Indonesia's 'People of the Forest.'" *National Geographic,* Vol. 148, No. 4, October, 1975.

MacKinnon, John, *In Search of the Red Ape.* New York: Holt, Rinehart & Winston, Inc., 1974.

Morison, Samuel Eliot, *The European Discovery of America: The Southern Voyages, 1492–1616.* New York: Oxford University Press, Inc., 1974. (Contains an excellent account of the passage of Magellan's fleet through the islands of the Malay Archipelago.)

Schultze-Westrum, Thomas, G., "A National Park System for Papua and New Guinea." *IUCN Bulletin,* New Series, Vol. 2, No. 16, July/September, 1970.

Wallace, Alfred Russell, *The Malay Archipelago: The Land of the Orang-utan and the Bird of Paradise.* London: Macmillan and Co., Ltd., 1922. (First printed in 1869.)

7   Australia, Strange Land Down Under

Bergamini, David, and the Editors of *Life, The Land and Wild-life of Australia*. New York: Time, Inc., 1964. (Includes material on New Guinea and New Zealand.)

Keast, Allen, *Australia and the Pacific Islands*. New York: Random House, Inc., 1966.

Russell, Franklin, "Death in Australia." *Audubon,* Vol. 76, No. 2, March, 1974.

Serventy, Vincent, *A Continent in Danger*. London: Andre Deutsch, Ltd., 1966.

Stivens, Dal, "The Thylacine Mystery." *Animal Kingdom,* Vol. 76, No. 3, June, 1973.

Troughton, Ellis, *Furred Animals of Australia*. New York: Charles Scribner's Sons, 1947.

8   New Zealand, Land of Flightless Birds

Carlquist, Sherman, *Island Life: A Natural History of the Islands of the World*. Garden City, New York: Natural History Press, 1965.

Darwin, Charles, *The Voyage of the Beagle*. New York: P. F. Collier & Son, 1909. The Harvard Classics edition. (First printed in London, 1839.)

Roedelberger, F. A. and Groschoff, Vera I., *Wildlife of the South Seas*. English version by Peter J. Whitehead. New York: The Viking Press, 1967.

Sidney, John, "New Zealand's Rare Birds: Threatened Species Breed at a Mountain Reserve." *Animal Kingdom,* Vol. 72, No. 6, December, 1969.

Waddick, James W., "The Tuatara." *Animal Kingdom*. Vol. 76, No. 5, October, 1973.

9   What Is the Future for Wildlife?

Dasmann, Raymond F., *The Last Horizon*. New York: Collier Books, 1971.

Dorst, Jean, *Before Nature Dies*. New York: Houghton Mifflin Company, 1970.

Falk, Richard A., *This Endangered Planet*. New York: Random House, Inc., 1971.

Scheffer, Victor B., *A Voice for Wildlife*. New York: Charles Scribner's Sons, 1974.

Ward, Barbara and Dubos, René, *Only One Earth: The Care and Maintenance of a Small Planet*. New York: W. W. Norton & Company, Inc., 1972.

Zimmerman, David R., *To Save a Bird in Peril*. New York: Coward McCann & Geohegan, Inc., 1975.

SECTION II

Exploration and Discovery in the Old World

Armstrong, Richard, *The Discoverers*. New York: Praeger Publishers, Inc., 1968.

Cary, M., and Warmington, E. H., *The Ancient Explorers*. London: Methuen & Co., Ltd., 1929.

Gillespie, James Edward, *A History of Geographical Discovery, 1400–1800*. New York: Henry Holt and Company, 1933.

Emory, Kenneth P., "The Coming of the Polynesians." *National Geographic,* Vol. 146, No. 6, December, 1974.

Hyde, Walter Woodburn, *Ancient Greek Mariners*. New York: Oxford University Press, 1947.

Stefansson, Vilhjalmur, *Great Adventures and Explorations*. New York: The Dial Press, 1947.

Sykes, Percy, *A History of Exploration from the Earliest Times to the Present Day*. London: George Routledge & Sons, Ltd., 1934.

Wright, Louis B., *Gold, Glory, and the Gospel*. New York: Atheneum Publishers, 1970.

Man's Effect on Land and Wildlife of All Continents

Amory, Cleveland, *Man Kind?: Our Incredible War on Wildlife.* New York: Harper & Row, Publishers, 1974.

Crandall, Lee S., *The Management of Wild Animals in Captivity.* Chicago: The University of Chicago Press, 1964.

Crowe, Philip Kingsland, *The Empty Ark.* New York: Charles Scribner's Sons, 1967.

————, *World Wildlife, the Last Stand.* New York: Charles Scribner's Sons, 1971.

Curry-Lindahl, Kai, *Let Them Live: A Worldwide Survey of Animals Threatened with Extinction.* New York: William Morrow & Company, Inc., 1972.

Edinburgh, the Duke of, and Fisher, James, *Wildlife Crisis.* New York: Cowles Book Company, Inc., 1970.

Fisher, James, Simon, Noel, and Vincent, Jack, *Wildlife in Danger.* New York: The Viking Press, 1969.

Gary, Romain and the Editors of Time-Life Books, *Vanishing Species.* New York: Time-Life Books, 1974.

Greenway, James C., *Extinct and Vanishing Birds of the World.* New York: American Committee for International Wildlife Protection, 1958.

Guggisberg, C. A. W., *Man and Wildlife.* New York: Arco Publishing Company, Inc., 1970.

Harper, Francis, *Extinct and Vanishing Mammals of the Old World.* New York: American Committee for International Wildlife Protection, 1945.

Heuvelmans, Bernard, *On the Track of Unknown Animals.* New York: Hill & Wang, 1959.

Hornaday, William Temple, *Our Vanishing Wildlife: Its Extermination and Preservation.* New York: Charles Scribner's Sons, 1913.

Huxley, Sir Julian, Consultant Ed., *The Rand McNally Atlas of*

World Wildlife. New York: Rand McNally & Company, 1973.

International Zoo Yearbook, Vols. 1–15. London: The Zoological Society of London, 1960–1975.

IUCN Bulletin, New Series. Switzerland: IUCN (International Union for Conservation of Nature and Natural Resources), Vol. 2, No. 6 (January/March, 1968) through Vol. 6, No. 12 (December, 1975).

IUCN Red Data Books: Vol. 1. *Mammalia,* compiled by Goodwin, Harry A. and Holloway, Colin W., 1972, with additional sheets through 1974; Vol. 2. *Aves,* compiled by Vincent, Jack, 1966, with additional sheets through 1971; Vol. 3. *Amphibia and Reptilia,* compiled by Honegger, René E., 1968, with additional sheets through 1970. Switzerland: IUCN.

King, F. Wayne, "Slaughter of the Wild." *Animal Kingdom,* Vol. 78, No. 2, April/May, 1975.

Milne, Lorus J. and Margery, *The Cougar Doesn't Live Here Anymore.* Englewood Cliffs, New Jersey: Prentice-Hall, Inc., 1971.

Mochi, Ugo, and Carter, Donald T., *Hoofed Mammals of the World.* New York: Charles Scribner's Sons, 1953.

Regenstein, Lewis, *The Politics of Extinction: The Shocking Story of the World's Endangered Wildlife.* New York: The Macmillan Publishing Company, Inc., 1975.

Silverberg, Robert, *The Auk, the Dodo, and the Oryx: Vanished and Vanishing Creatures.* New York: Thomas Y. Crowell Company, Inc., 1967.

Simon, Noel M. and Geroudet, Paul, *Last Survivors: Natural History of 48 Animals in Danger of Extinction.* New York and Cleveland: World Publishing Company, Inc., 1970.

Stivens, Dal, *The Incredible Egg: A Billion Year Journey.* New York: Weybright & Talley, Inc., 1974.

Topsell, Edward, *The History of Four-Footed Beasts and Ser-*

pents and Insects. Vol. 1, the History of four-footed beasts, taken principally from the *Historia Animalium* of Conrad Gesner. With a new introduction by Willy Ley. New York: Da Capo Press, 1967. (An unabridged republication of the 1658 edition published in London.)

INDEX
* indicates illustration

279